DUTCHER FAMILY:

OUR

COLONIAL ANCESTORS

AND THEIR

DESCENDANTS.

HISTORICAL, GENEALOGICAL, BIOGRAPHICAL.

COMPILES BY

HENRY WHITTEMORE

JANAWAY PUBLISHING, INC.
Santa Maria, California

Notice

In many older books, foxing (or discoloration) occurs and, in some instances, print lightens with wear and age. Reprinted books, such as this, often duplicate these flaws, notwithstanding efforts to reduce or eliminate them. The pages of this reprint have been digitally enhanced and, where possible, the flaws eliminated in order to provide clarity of content and a pleasant reading experience.

Dutcher Family: Our Colonial Ancestors and Their Descendants

Compiled by:

Henry Whittemore

Originally published:
Watertown, N. Y.
1902

Reprinted by

Janaway Publishing, Inc.
732 Kelsey Ct.
Santa Maria, California 93454
(805) 925-1038
www.janawaygenealogy.com

2016

ISBN: 978-1-59641-213-2

S. B. Dutcher

OUR

COLONIAL ANCESTORS

AND THEIR

DESCENDANTS.

HISTORICAL, GENEALOGICAL, BIOGRAPHICAL.

COMPILED BY

HENRY WHITTEMORE,

Author of the Genealogical Guide to the Early Settlers of America, and other works.

PRINTED BY
THE HUNGERFORD-HOLBROOK CO.
Watertown, N. Y
1902.

DISCOVERY AND SETTLEMENT OF NEW NETHER-LANDS OR NEW YORK.

Unlike the settlement of the New England colonies which began through religious persecution, that of New York and other Middle States began through the commercial enterprise of merchants of the Old World.

Hendrick Hudson, an Englishman, sailing in the employ of Holland merchants, started on his voyage of discovery in the "Half-Moon," April 6, 1609, from Amsterdam, and came to anchor in the "Great River of the Mountains," September 11, 1609. He ascended the river as far as Albany, and after formally taking possession of the whole domain which he had discovered in the name of the States-General of Holland, he sailed for England.

Upon the announcement of these discoveries at home, the enterprising merchants of North Holland, under whose auspices they had been made, united themselves into a company and received from the States-General a special trading-license or charter, dated October 11, 1614. This document, in which the name of "New Netherland"

first appears officially in the world's annals, invested the "United New Netherlands Company" with the exclusive right of "visiting and trading in the newly discovered lands lying in America between New France and Virginia, the seacost whereof extends from the fortieth to the forty-fifth degrees of latitude, for four voyages within the period of three years from the first of January next ensuing or sooner."

The organization of the company was delayed by various causes for a period of two years, when its articles of internal regulations, the charter having in the interval been somewhat modified, were formally approved by the States-General June 21, 1623.

Warned by the evident and growing jealousy of the English, the West Indian Company (by which name it was now known) lost no time, even before their final organization, in securing in the year 1622 their title to New Netherland by taking formal possession, and by making arrangements for the building of two new forts, one on the North River to be called "Fort Orange," and the other called "Fort Nassau," in the South or Delaware River, near the present town of Gloucester, N. J. And simultaneously with the final organization in June, 1623, the company began the colonization of New Netherland, which was erected into a province and invested with the armorial bearings of a count. This was a shield bearing a beaver proper, surrounded by a count's coronet, and inscribed by the legend, "*Sigillum Iovi Belgil.*"

The management of its affairs was entrusted to the Amsterdam Chambers, which sent out the ship "New Netherland" with a company of thirty families, mostly Walloons, under the care of Captain Cornelius Jacobson May, of Hoorn, who was appointed the first director of the colony. In 1625, two ships, with a stock of cattle, farming utensils, seeds and other necessaries, with forty-five emigrants, together with their families, arrived in the new colony. William Verhulst succeeded May in the directorship, and in 1626 Peter Minuet, as Director General or Governor of the Province, arrived with other settlers, and purchased the island of Manhattan from the Indians for seventy guilders (about $24), and a large fort was erected at its lower end and named "Fort Amsterdam."

On June 7, 1629, a "Charter of Freedoms and Exemptions" was adopted, which was approved and confirmed by the States-General. In this charter the company, with the purpose of encouraging independent colonists, offered to such the absolute property of as much land as each could "properly improve." Any member who should plant a company of fifty adults in any part of New Netherland, except Manhattan Island, which the company reserved to itself, should be acknowledged as the "patroon," or feudal chief of such a colony or territory with the high and low jurisdictions, the exclusive rights of fishing, hunting and grinding, etc., within his own domain; to which, also, he was to have a full title of inheritance, with right of disposing of it by will at his death.

Several parties availed themselves of this opportunity to acquire patroonships, among these Blommaert and Godyn in the South River, Van Rensselaer on the North River, Pauw at Hoboken, Hacking and Pavonia (now Jersey City) and Staten Island. In the summer of 1632, the company despatched commissaries to each settlement to post up their proclamation forbidding any person, whether patroon or vassal, to deal in sewan, peltries or maize.

Those who were sent to Fort Orange were Bastiaen Jansen Krol, Commissary, and Dierck Cornslissen Duyster, Under Commissary.

DUTCHER FAMILY.

DE DUYSTER, (DUCHIER), OR DUTCHER AND ALLIED FAMILIES.

In all the early church records of New York State, this name is spelt in nearly every instance with "De", as De Duyster, De Duyscher, De Dautscher, etc., clearly indicating its French origin.

The tradition is that the family went from France to Holland during the early part of the 16th century. The following record is found in "Livre D'or de Noblesse" 451, 4th Register, a work on French Heraldry, containing a history of many of the noble families of France:

"En 1679 Gilbert de Saincthorent figure dans un acte comme fils de Robert de Saincthorent seigneur de Faye, et de damoiselle GILBERT DUCHIER, fille noble de Jean Duchier, seigneur de la Courcille."

(In 1679 Gilbert de Saincthorent appeared as the son of Robert de Saincthorent, Lord of Fay (or Lord Fay), and a noble damsel, daughter of Jean Duchier, Lord of the Council.)

Duchier or Dutcher.

ARMS DE DUCHIER. D'azur d'une grue d'or tenant un vigilance d'argent, et un chief d'or, charge de trois roses de gueules.

(Arms of Duchier. Azure a crane or, holding a stone (argent) in claw—a chief, charged with three roses gules.)

The crane holding the stone in its claws indicates vigilance, that is, should the crane incline to sleep, the stone drops from its claws, and the bird instantly awakes. The motto, "Thorns encompass the roses," carries its own definition.

Other French works contain references to the Duchier family, which is the only one that appears in any way to correspond with the De Duister or De Duytscher family, the pronunciation of the latter closely resembling that of Duchier.

From the Dictionaire History de la Noblesse p. 1076 "Famille originain de Saintonge sur laquelle les renseignements font defaut."

From Poplement la France Heraldique vol. I, 259, "Cette famille a pour seul representaut Duchier de Jupille directerer du depot des etalons a Allencon."

The first mention of the name of Duyster or De Duyster in the New York records is that of Dierck Cornellissen Duyster, Under, or Assistant Commissary at Fort Orange.

O'Callahan's History of New Netherlands contains the following:

"April 18, 1630.   Other wealthy and influential directors of the company hastened now to become patroons also, and early in the following spring, Bastian Jansen Krol, Commissary, and DIERCK COR-NELISSEN DUYSTER, Under Commissary, at Fort Orange, having learned that a tract of land called Sannahagog, lying on the west side of the North River, extending from Beren Island, and in breadth two days' journey was for sale, purchased the same from Paep Sekenekomplas Nancouttanshal and Seckoussen, the native proprietors, for Killian Van Rensselaer, a pearl merchant in Amsterdam, and one of the directors of the West India Company.

"Nearly seven years afterwards—namely, on the 13th of April, 1637, an intervening district called Papsickinckas or Papsekenea, as the name is now pronounced, lying also on the east bank of the river and extending from opposite Castle Island south to the point opposite Smackx Island, and including the adjacent islands, and all the lands back into the interior belonging to the Indian owner's, was purchased 'for certain quantities of duffels, axes, knives, and wampum' also for Mr. Van Ransselaer, who thus became proprietor of a tract of country twenty-four miles long and forty-eight miles broad, containing as is estimated seven hundred thousand acres of land, which now comprises the counties of Albany, Rensselaer, and part of the county of Columbia.

"The names of the Director, Minuet, Bastian Jansen Krol, DIERCK CORNELISZ DUYSTER, Peter Byvelt, Jan Lampo (schout), Rynert Harmenssen, Jan Janssen Myndertz, are signed to the first of these deeds, which is certified by Leonard Cole, Assistant Secretary, in the absence of Jan Van Remund, Secretary. The other instrument is signed by Peter Minuet, Director, Peter Byvelt, Jacob Elbertzen Weissing, Jan Jansen Brouwer, Simon Dircksen Pos, Raynner Harmenz, Samuel Cole, Assistant Secretary, in the absence of the Secretary, with the seal of New Netherlands in red wax." Copies of all these deeds are in the Book of Patent Office of the Secretary of State, G. G. 13, 14, 15, 16, 23, 24, 25, 26, and among the Rensselaerwyck Mss. See also Holland Doc. I, 181, 184."

No baptismal records of the Reformed Dutch Church have been found earlier than 1683, and these are doubtless imperfect. Copies of these baptismal records 1683 to 1695 are published in Munsell's Annals of Albany, vol. III, in which the following De Duyster or De Duytcher appear.

Johannes bap. Sep. 21, 1701.

Christena, daughter of Roelof de Duytcher and Jannilje Brisse, Sponsor, Class Brisse, Antji Brisse, 1703.

Cristoffel, son of Roelof de Duyster, Sponsors, Andries Bressy, Hester Wendel.

All the baptismal records after the above are found in the Kingston Reformed Dutch Church, that town being at the time a part of Albany County, and the same dominie officiating at both churches. The following names have been copied from the Kingston baptismal records and grouped together so as to show the children of each family.

I Margaret, dau. of Derrick de Duyster, bap. Sep. 15, 1700.

II Johannes, son, Dirk de Duyster, Jannetje Bont, Oct. 4, 1702.

III Henricus, son, Dirk de Duitscher, Jannetje Bont, Sep. 3, 1704.

IV Lea, dau. Dirck de Duyster, Jannitji Bront, Dec. 1, 1706.

V David, son Dirk Duidser, Janne Brondt, Sept. 16, 1709.
　　Witnesses.　David de Duidser, Maritji Wells.

VI Cornelis, son, Dirk de Duyster, Jannitji Bront, June 17, 1711.
　　Witness.　Corn. de Duyster, Cornelia de Duyster.

VII Catrina, dau. Dirk de Duytscher, Jannitji Bont, Feb. 7, 1714.

VIII Rachel, dau. Dirk de Duyser, Jannetjen Bont, May 18, 1717.

IX Maria, dau Dirk de Duytscher, Jannetjen Bont, July 5, 1719.

I Johannes, son of Roelof de Duyster, Jannitje Bressie, Sept. 21, 1701.

II Margariet, dau. Roelof de Duidser, Jannitji Bressy, May 7, 1710. Witnesses. David de Duidser, Maria Wels.

Margaret, dau. of David de Duytscher, Leonard de Hoges, April 23, 1693.

Richard, son of Jan Wels, Cornelia de Duyster, June 8, 1694.

Jan, son of Jan Wels, Cornelia de Duyster, Dec. 28, 1701.

Samuel, son of Jan Wels, Cornelia de Duyster, March 12, 1704.

Johannes, son of Jan Roelan, Catharine de Duyster, April 13, 1701.

Joel, son of Jan Roclan, Catharine de Duyster, Jan. 7, 1703.

Lucas, son of Catrina de Duyster, Father not named, June 3, 1694.

This last is probably the same Catharine who afterwards became the wife of Jan Roelan.

Rachel, dau. of Johannes de Duytser, Catrina Bogardus, May 21, 1727.   Witnesses, Cornelius and Rachel Bogardus.

Lydia, dau. of Johannes de Duyster, Catrina Bogardus, Dec. 1, 1728.   "Bp'd over the River" (Rhinebeck.)

Dirk, son of Johannes de Duyster, Catrina Bogardus, May 5, 1730. Witnesses, David de Duyster, Aaianiji Vriedenburg. "Bp'd in Rynbeck."

Jannitji, dau. of Johannes de Duyster, Catrina Bogardus.

Jeremias, son of Johannes de Duyster, Catrina Bogardus, Dec. 1, 1734.

Catrina, dau of Johannes de Duyster, Catrina Bogardus, July 12, 1741.

Zara, child of Johannes de Duyster, Catrina Bogardus, Jan. 31, 1748.

Johannes, son of John Oosteroom, Magteltji de Duyster, Aug. 15, 1703.

Cornelis, son of Jacob Westervelt, Margaret de Duyster, Sept. 20, 1723.

Elizabeth, dau. of Jacob Westervelt, June 16, 1726.

Jacob, son of Jacob Westervelt, Margaret de Duyster, June 19, 1734.   Bap. in Minisink.

Catrina, dau. of Jacobus Von Sternbergen, Grietjin de Duyster, Sept. 26, 1725.

Jennokin, son of Jacobus Von Sternbergen, Grietjin de Duyster, Nov. 26, 1727.

Zara, child of Jacobus Von Strenbergen, Grietji de Duyster, Oct. 1, 1728.

A child of Jacobus Van Strenbergen, March 29, 1730.

Cornelius de Duyster is the first of the name found on the records of Albany and Ulster counties after that of Dirk Cornelissen Duyster the Commissary. There is strong collateral evidence to support the theory that this second Cornelius was the son of the Commissary of Fort Orange. The History of Ulster County contains the following:

"A rool of the names and surnames of them that have taken the oath of allegiance in ye county of Ulstr by ordr of his excely ye governor ye ffirst day of September Anno Qc Domini 1689.

"There ffolowing persons Did nott appear, viz.

Cornelius ye Duitcher (and others named.)"

Ulster County was formed November 1st, 1683. In its charter, it is said to contain the towns of Kingston, Hurley and Marbletown, Foxhall and the New Paltz and all villages, neighborhoods and Christian habitations on the west side of the Hudson River from the Murderer's Creek near the highlands to the Sawyer's Creek. Kingston was incorporated by patent May 19, 1667, New Paltz was granted by patent by Gov. Andros, Sept. 29, 1677, Marbletown was formed by patent June 26, 1703. The town of Hurley lies just west of the territory of Kingston, south by Rosendale and Marbletown and west by Marbletown and Olive. On June 7, 1663, Hurley, then known as New Village, was attacked by the Indians and entirely burned. The majority of the people were made captives. The population being only 174, thirty-seven years afterwards, proves that not very rapid progress had been made; that Rochester and Marbletown had increased faster than Hurley. The records of the town have been lost. The earliest dates back to 1720.

With few exceptions, the earliest church records of Albany and Ulster counties are found at Kingston and the Kingston Reformed Dutch Church contains most of the data found of the Dutcher or De Duyster family.

A mortgage dated March 10, 1692-3, from Cornelius de Duyster and Leonard, his wife, of Hurley, to William Fisher, conveyed land belonging to Jan Gavitse (probably son of Adrian Gavitse, one of the patentees of Hurley) and by him sold to Wm. de La Montagne, former husband of Leonord de Duyster, in Monbackus, (A. A. of Deeds, 120). Johannes de La Montague was a Huguenot and was Vice Director and Deputy at Fort Orange. William was his son; Leonora, his wife, above mentioned, was Leonora de Hooges, daughter of Anthony, who died about 1656, and her mother took her family with her at the Esopus and married Roelof Swartwout in 1657. (This Swartwout was also one of the patentees of Hurley). Leonora had seven children by de La Montagne, the first born July 2, 1674, the last July 28, 1688.

MILITARY RECORD.

Report of State Historian of New York, page 441, shows that "David de Duyster and Roelof de Duyster were members in July, 1711, of Capt. Wessil ten Broeck's Company of Ulster County.

558, Cornelius de Duyster, member of Capt. Johannes Vernooy's Company, enlisted 1715.

Dirk de Duyster was a member of Johannes Shipman's Company of militia of the town of Hurley, 1715.

415, Dirk de Duyster was in the roll of men of Major Peter Schuyler's Company 1692, detached out of the counties of Westchester, Richmond, Kings, Queens, Suffolk and Ulster.

523, Reference is made to the Independent Company of the Manor of Livingston, as they were "mustered at ye manor house on the 30th day of November, 1715."

William White, Sergeant.

Gabriel Brussie.

Lawrence Knickerbocker.

Roelof de Duyster.

George White.

This CORNELIUS DE DUYSTER was, no doubt, a resident of Hurley, in Ulster county, and the father of Dirk, or Derrick, Roelof, David, Cornelius (3), and other children.   He was evidently named after Cornelius, his father, and in naming his eldest child Dirk, after his father, also was the usual custom of perpetuating the name of the ancestor.   It was also custom among the Dutch when a child was named after the grandfather, for the grandparents to appear as witnesses or sponsors.   At the baptism of Cornelius, sixth child of Dirk de Duyster, the witnesses were "Corn de Duyster and Cornila de Duyster."   These were, no doubt, parents of the following, whose record of marriage is shown in the Kingston Church Records:

"Nov. 19, 1699, Derrick de Duyster, jen, born and resides in Horley (Hurley), and Jannitji Bont, ja, born in s'Kingtde (Schenectady) and resides in Horley (Hurley).

Banns published but dates not given.

Nov. 17, 1700, Roelof de Duyster, jen, born in Moomelt (Marbletown), and Jannitji Bressie, ja, born in Albanien (Albany) and both reside in Kingston."

Banns published but dates not given.

"Feb. 19, 1714, David de Duyscher, jen, born in the 'Esopus or Kingston.' Banns registered 2nd June.

"June 24, 1726. Johannes de Duyster, jen, born in Horley (Hurley) and Catrina Bogardus born in Kingston an both of their Banns registered 5th June."

The names of those who appear to have been brothers and sisters of the above and others children of each are found in the Kingston Records. Descendants of Dirk de Duyster are found in Dutchess and adjoining counties.

David, Roelof and Dirck de Duyster settled within a short distance of each other in Dutchess County. Roelof settled in what is now Dover Plains and Dirck or Derrick at what is now Wing Station in South Dover. All this was then comprised in the Livingston Manor a part of which bordered on the State of Connecticut. David settled on the Rombout Patent at what was one time known as Freedom, now La Grange, about ten miles distant from Dover Plains. It will thus be seen that three of the supposed brothers settled within a short distance of each other.

Cornelius de Duytcher (3) settled in Minisink, Orange County, as appears by the Calendar of New York Historical Manuscripts, vol. II, p. 447.

"Nov. 9, 1719. Petition of Nicklas Westfall, Johannes Westfall, Teunis Quick, CORNELIUS DE DUYSTER, Simon Westfall, Rymeny Quick of the County of Orange, setting forth that Thomas Beonardus, Jacob and Roelof Swartworst and others to the number of 36 persons trespassed on their lands lying at Wayhackmeck on the little Minnesing Creek in said county."

LINE OF ROELOF DE DUYSTER, SUPPOSED SON OF CORNELIUS, SON OF DIERCK CORNELIUS DUYSTER.

Roelof de Duyster, supposed son of Cornelius (who was probably son of Dierck Cornelius) was born in Mormelt (Marbleton) near Kingston, N.Y., about 1670. He married at Kingston (banns published Nov. 17, 1700) Jannetji Bressie, born in Albany, but at that time residing in Kingston. In July, 1711, he was a member of an Ulster County regiment, commanded by Capt. Wessels Ten Broeck. On Nov. 30, 1715, he was a private in the "Independent Companies of the Manor of Livingston as mustered at ye manor house." After leaving Ulster County he resided at Dover Plains, which was then a part of the Livingston Manor.

In the History of Dutchess County, page 60, is shown a list of the inhabitants and slaves in the county of Dutchess in 1714:

Roelof Dutcher. His family consisted of 1 male between 16 and 60 years of age.

3 males under 16.

2 females between 16 and 60.

1 female under 16.

1 slave.

The History of Litchfield County, Conn., states that "Three Dutch families from the Livingston Manor in the province of New York, commenced the settlement of Weatogue (the Indian name for Salisbury). Their lands were purchased of William Gaylord and Stephen Noble of New Milford by deeds dated Aug. 29, 1720. The names of Roelof and wife appear as late as July 26, 1722, upon the records of the Dutch Church at Kingston as witnesses at the baptism of Jannitjen, daughter of Josua (Joshua) Weyt (White) and Christina Duyster, his wife. This Joshua White was a son of Sergeant William White.

The Dutchers settled upon land still further north and extending to the State line in the town of Salisbury on the Housatonic River. While the last representative of the family has departed from this locality,

THE OLD DUTCHER BRIDGE

which spans the Housatonic River from Salisbury to Canaan still remains as an ancient landmark to mark the locality.

THE OLD DUTCHER BRIDGE ON THE HOUSATONIC RIVER ERECTED 1760
BETWEEN SALISBURY AND CANAAN CONN

The History of Litchfield County, Connecticut, states that "The first bridge erected across the Housatonic River was the Falls Bridge, for many years known as Barral's Bridge. This bridge was built about 1744. Dutcher's Bridge was erected in 1760.

"Previous to the act of incorporation," says Judge Church, "there were no public roads here, yet there were some well defined paths. The most prominent among these was the one leading from Dutcher's in Weatogue.

"The first recorded survey of a highway was made Nov. 6, 1744, from Gabriel Dutcher's in the northeast section of the town to Benjamin White's; another the same year from Cornelius Knickerbocker's at the Furnace to Samuel Billows's at the eastern foot of Smith's Hill."

A writer in the History of Litchfield County, referring to this locality, says: "In investigating some titles some years ago of land in Wetauge, I found the prominent description of one corner of a tract to Christopher's canoe place. I infer therefore that this was a well-known crossing, and near the present residence of Ruloff Dutcher in Canaan, whose ancestor was Christopher Dutcher."

The following is a copy of the deed of land.

"New Milford, August 29, 1720, Roulef Dutcher, deed.

"Know all men by these presents that we William Gaylord and Stephen Noble both of New Milford in the County of Newhaven and Colony of Connecticut In New England for and in consideration of forty-two pounds current money of New-York which is to our full satisfaction and contentments have Given Granted Bargained and sold and by these presents do fully freely firmly and absolutely Grant Bargain and sell unto Roeluf Dutcher of weatauck in the colony of Connecticut his heirs and assigns a certain parcell of land lying at that place called weatack within the bound of Connecticut colony by estimation one hundred and fifty acres butted and bounded as followeth southerly and easterly upon the great River the southwest corner a black oacke spire the line from this spire running east to the ege of a swamp and from thence south to the turn of the river; north and west upon undivided land together with all the privileges and appurtenances thereunto belonging to have and to hold to him the said Roulef Dutcher his heirs and assigns for ever as a free Indefezable estate of inheritance for ever; and further we the sd william Gaylord and Stephen Noble for ourselves our heirs and assigns do covenant and promise to alinate the same and that he and they shall quietly and peaceably have hold and Injoy all the above bargained premises without let or molestation from us our heirs or assigns affirming ourselves to be the true and lawful owners of the above bargained premises and lawfully seized of the same and that he and they shall quitly and peaceably Injoy the same without let or molestation from us or our heirs in witnes whereof we have set it to our hand and seall this twenty ninth of august 1720.

Signed sealed in presence of

Sam^{ll} Brownson

Abram Vandusa
his X mark

William Gaylord   Seal

Stephen Noble   Seal

New Milford, August 29, 1720.

then personally appeared William Gaylord and Stephen Noble both of New Milford and acknowledged the within written instrument to be their free and voluntary act and deed.

Before me Sam^{ll} Brownson Justice.

State of Connecticut, }
County of Litchfield, } ss.   Town Clerk's Office, New Milford.

The foregoing is a true copy from Vol. 2, pages 176, 177 of the Land Records, in this office.

Seal.   (Signed) Russel B. Noble, Town Clerk.

The first town meeting convened in 1739, at "Mr. Christopher Dutcher's dwelling house on ye 19th day of this Instant, Desember at 12 of the clock on said day." In the descriptions in a number of early deeds appear the following: "Dutcher's path in Weatogue;" and "Christopher Dutcher's canoe place." The grand-list in 1742 of the taxable property contains the following entries:

Henry Dutcher	49lb	08
Christopher Dutcher	9	5
Ruluff	60	14
John	74	18
Gabriel	74	0
Cornelius	54	6
Widow	42	10

The within is a true list as it was given to us.

Ruluff Dutcher.

*   *   *

*   *   *

Assessors for ye year 1742.

ROELOFF DE DUYSTER, the ancestor of this branch of the family, was born probably about 1670, died January 19, 1737. The widow, Jannetje Dutcher, died July 26, 1749. He was an industrious and thrifty farmer, and left a family which proved a credit to him and to the town of which he was the chief founder, as shown by the records.

He married Jannitji Bressie of Albany County, N. Y., whose ancestor was no doubt among the early French Refugees who fled from France to Holland during the fifteenth or sixteenth centuries. They had issue:

I. Johannes, bap. Sept. 21, 1701, at Kingston, died young.

II. Christina, bap. Aug. 8, 1703, at Albany; married Joshua Weyt (White) and had Jennitjen, bap. July 1, 1722, at Kingston.

II. Christophel, bap. July 15, 1705, at Albany.

IV. *Johannes*, bap. Jan. 25, 1708, at Albany.

V. Margaret, bap. May 7, 1710, at Kingston.

VI. Cornelius, born about 1712.

VII. Ruluff, born about 1716.

VIII *Gabriel*, born July 15, 1720.

ESTATE OF RULOOF DUTCHERS.

Att a Court of Probate held in Woodbury, June 9th, 1737, Mr. Christopher Dutchers of Weataug come and appeared in Court and Exhibited ye Last Will or Testament of Mr. Ruloof Dutchers late of Weataug (who deceased about ye 19th of January last past) in order to its approbation; wc matter was weighed by ye Court and sd Will was allowed and approved and ordered to be Recorded and is as followeth:

And whereas the Testator in said Testament appointed his beloved wife Jonyche and his eldest son Christopher Executrix and Executor of sd Testament, on ye date above sd Christopher Dutchers before ye Court declared his acceptance of sd care and himself bound to Joseph Minor, Esqr. Judge of ye Probate in Woodbury & his Lawful successors in a Recognizance of five Hundred pounds Current money of New England that he will be faithful unto ye above Trust.

Attest

ANTHONY STODDARD, Clerk.

THE WILL.

In the Name of God, Amen, the Seventeenth day of January A. D. 1736-7, I Ruloof Dutchers of Weataug in Connecticut, Husbandman, being infirm & weak in body but of perfect mind & memory, Thanks be given to God; Therefore calling to mind the Mortallity of my body and knowing that the Grave is the house appointed for all Living, and yt by ye Statute of Heaven it is appointed for all men once to die, Do make and ordain this my last Will and Testament, that is to say, principally and first of all, I Give and Recommend my Soul into the hands of God that gave it, and my Body I Recommend to the Earth to be buried in decent Christian buriall, at ye discretion of my Executors, Nothing doubting but at the general Resurrection I shall receive the same again by ye mighty power of God; and as touching such worldly Estate wherewith it hath pleased God to bless me in this life, I give, demise, and dispose of ye same in the following manner:

Imprimis.   I Give and Bequeath to Jonyche my dearly beloved wife the whole of my estate, real and personal, during her life, Excepting a negro girl whose name is Sarah, which girl I give to Catreene my Daughter.

Item.   I give to my well beloved son Christopher, twelve shillings.

Item.   I give to Cristeene, my well beloved Daughter, One Hundred Pounds in Money to be paid out of my Estate in four years after the death of me and my wife.

Item.   I give to my well beloved son, Gabriel, my Mansion House and Barn & Orchard and the whole of my house lot, he paying thirty pounds to his brothers and sisters, or to my estate, within six years after my decease.

Item. I give to my well beloved Sons and Daughters, (viz.) Christopher, Johannis, Cornelius, Ruloof, Gabriel, & Margeret & Catreene, the whole of my Estate, Real and personal, (excepting what I have given to my sons Christopher and Gabriel and daughters Christeene) to be divided to them in Equal proportions after the decease of me and my Wife.

Moreover I Give my Wearing Cloaths, and all my Instruments for ye carrying on of Husbandry to my sons to be divided equally among them, and my Wive's Wearing Cloaths together with my beds and bedding to my two daughters Margerett & Catreene to be equall divided between them, and as to my household stuff, or the furniture of my house, it is to be equally divided among them, Christeene excepted, and Gabriel shall have my best handirons; and my stock, Horses and Cattle, etc., It shall be divided equally among my children, Christeene excepted.

And I give my children my Estate in manner & form aforesd with this Limitation, or upon this Condition, that if any one or more of them be reduced to poverty and be obliged to sell their part or parts, that the rest of my children shall have it, if they will give as much as a Stranger. And if my Estate be in debt, then I Will and appoint that ye debts be paid out of my whole Estate, each Child to pay an equal part, Cristeene excepted, who is to pay nothing.

Moreover, I give my Negros, Men, Women, and Children (excepting Sarah wc I gave to Catreene) to my children, to be divided epually among them, Christeen excepted, And I do make, constitute & ordain my well beloved Wife & my Son Christopher Executors of this my last will and Testament; and I do hereby utterly Disallow Revoke and Disannul all and every other former Testaments, Wills, Legacies, & Bequests and Executors by me in any way before named,

Willed & bequeathed, Ratifying and Confirming this and no other to be my last Will & Testament.

In Witness whereof I have hereunto set my hand and Seal, the day and year above written.

Ruloof Dutchers.   (L.S.)

X

his mark

Signed, Sealed, Published, pronounced & declared by the sd Ruloof Dutchers as his last Will and Testament in presence of us ye subscribers.

his

Jacob IP Plough

mark

his

Godfrey VD Vandarser

mark

Jonathan Hubbard.

Octbr. 24th, 1737, ye Executor of ye above Will, viz. Christopher Dutchers came and took ye Will and ye business out of this Office, his Counsel leading him so to do, apprehending it not well consisting with Law to settle ye Estate in and by this Probate.

DISTRICT OF WOODBURY, }
  PROBATE COURT,   } ss: December 12, 1901.

I, James Huntington, Judge of said Probate Court, hereby certify that the foregoing is a true Copy of the Record of said Court as appears from Vol. 2 of its Records, pages 68 and 69 thereof.

In witness whereof I have hereunto set my hand and the Seal of said Court, the day and year above written.

(L.S.)   JAS. HUNTINGTON, Judge.

The town records of Salisbury, liber 4, page 367, contains the following details of a division of the Dutcher property among the brothers:

Whereas we, Christopher of Canaan in the county of Hartford, Colony of Connecticut, New England, and Johannes Dutcher, Cornelius Dutcher, Ruluff Dutcher and Gabriel Dutcher, all of Salisbury in the County of New Haven and Colony aforesaid, have all of us a share in the land lying in Salisbury, formerly known by the name of Weatauge, which our Honored Father Ruluff Dutcher Late of said Weatauge, Deceased Left to us his children to be Divided Equally amongst us Excepting the orchard and the Home Lott which piece is bounded North on a fence between orchard and the plowland, south on a fence, that is about eight rods southward of the House that our said Father Dwelt in East on a Cove and west on a swamp which piece by a Legacy in our said Father's Last Will and Testament, bearing Date January the seventeenth A. D. 1736, was given to Gabriel, as by sd will may appear therefor to the end that a perpetual portion and Division be had and made between us the Parties and each one of us should have our respective parts and proportions of all the above mentioned Lands (Excepting some swamps on the old Farm orchard without draining are useless and therefore for the present held in common amongst us) according to Quantity and Quality set forth to each one in Particular. [Here follows a description of the several plots or farms among the children, which covers six closely written pages, making probably three thousand words or more.]

N. B. Whereas the foregoing Instrument was Drawn at the time of the Date thereof and not executed and the above named Christopher deceased, we Herty Dutcher, wife of Deceased Christopher Dutcher, and Ruloff Dutcher, son of said Christopher Dutcher, both of Canaan in Litchfield County as heirs of the said Christopher Dutcher Deceased, with the Rest of the Subscribers have mutually agreed to execute the above Instrument in Salisbury, July the 24th A. D. 1758.

	her	
	Herty X Dutcher	( )
In presence of	mark	
Andrew Stevens	Ruluff Dutcher	( )
John Hutchinson	his	
Salisbury in Litchfield County July	John Dutcher X	( )
24, 1758, then Mrs. Herty Dutcher and	mark	
Ruluff Dutcher of Canaan and John	his	
Dutcher and Gabriel Dutcher, all sign-	Cornelius X Dutcher	( )
ers and sealers of the above Instrument,	mark	
personally appeared in said Salisbury,	Ruluff Dutcher	( )
and acknowledged the same to be their	Gabriel Dutcher	( )
Act and deed before me, John Hutch-		
inson, Justice of ye Peace.		

LINE OF JOHANNES DUTCHER, FOURTH CHILD OF ROLOEF AND JANNETJE BRESSIE.

Johannes Dutcher, fourth child of Ruloef, was bapt. at Albany, Jan. 25, 1708; married Christian _____, born 1717; they resided at Salisbury, Connecticut. Upon the records there his name is written John. "Christian, wife of John Dutcher, departed this life May 1, 1755, in the 39th year of her age.', His will is dated June 11, 1777. He devises to his sons John and Gabriel each the farm upon which each was living, besides bequests of personalty; to his daughters Jane, Hannah and Christian he bequeaths certain sums of money and other property, and makes them residuary legatees; to Gabriel he gives about fourteen acres of land "which lie in Sheffield, which I purchased of Noble Westerfield;" Gabriel is named as executor; John Landon, Tappan Beebe, and Ruluff White were the witnesses. The births of all their children are recorded upon the Salisbury town records.   Children:

I. Ruluff, born Sept. 15, 1741.   In April, 1760, a Ruluff Dutcher, born in Connecticut, was in Duchess Co., New York, and enlisted in Capt. Van Vechten's Co.

II. Jane, born Feb. 19, 1743; married ———— Sardam.

III. John, born June 2, 1745; married Jan., 1770, Lois Washburn, and they had children:

    1. Patience, born in Oblong, Dec. 22, 1770.

    2. John, born in Salisbury, Apr. 8, 1773.

    3. Phebe, born in Salisbury, Oct. 8, 1774.

    4. Lydia, born in Salisbury, Apr. 16, 1777.

IV. Gabriel, born June 16, 1747.

V. Hannah, born March 25, 1749; married Mar. 1, 1771. Ezekiel Fuller.

VI. Cornelius, born March 20, 1753; died Mar. 22, 1754.

VII. Christian, born Mar. 1, 1755; married ____ Beebe.

Gabriel Dutcher, fourth child of Johannes Dutcher (Ruluff (3) was born June 16, 1747; married Christine White.   Tradition says her surname was White.   She was born in 1750, and died June 23, 1818.   He died Oct. 22, 1820.   Following is a copy of his will:

"In the name of God amen:

"I, Gabriel Dutcher, of Salisbury in the County of Litchfield and State of Connecticut, being in health of body and of sound mind and memory, calling to mind my own mortality and knowing that it is appointed unto all men once to die, do make and ordain this my last will and testament in manner and form following, principally and first of all I recommend my soul to God who gave it me, trusting in the merits of his Son for His gracious acceptance, and my body I give to the earth from whence it was taken to be buried in a decent and christian manner, nothing doubting but I shall receive the same again by the mighty power God at the general resurrection a hope of eternal life, and with what worldly goods it hath pleased God to bless me with in this life I give and dispose of in the following manner (viz): My debts and funeral charges being first paid and discharged,

Imprimis I give and bequeath to my grandson Harry Dutcher, son of Lowrance Dutcher, deceased, to the said Harry Dutcher and to the heirs of his body one thousand dollars in land to be set off where it will be the least injury to the other heirs, also two hundred dollars in money, but if the said Harry should decease without natural heir or heirs then the aforesaid legacy of land and money to be equally divided between my two daughters Sarah Dickson and Catherine Deming, but provided my daughter Sarah Dickson should die without issue the said legacy to be given to the heirs of Catherine Deming, the said Catherine is to have the use and improvement thereof should the said Sarah decease aforesaid during her natural life.

Item. I give and bequeath to my three sisters, viz: Jane Sardam, Hannah Fuller and Christian Beebe to them and their heirs Fifty dollars to each of the said sisters making one hundred and fifty dollars in the whole.

Item. I give and bequeath to my daughter Sarah Dickson and to her heirs the one equal half of all my personal and real estate I am possessed of after my debts and the aforesaid legacies are paid and discharged, but if my said daughter Sarah Dickson should decease without issue or natural heirs then to the children of my daughter Catherine Deming the said Catherine is to have the use and improvement thereof should the said Sarah decease as aforesaid during her natural life.

Item. I give and bequeath to my daughter Catherine Deming and to her heirs the one equal half of all my personal and real estate I am possessed of which shall remain after my debts and the aforesaid legacies are paid and discharged.

Lastly I constitute and appoint Eliphalet Whittlesey the sole executor of this my last will and testament.

Signed, sealed, published and pronounced and declared by the said Gabriel Dutcher to be his last will and testament, who in our presence signed and sealed the same and in the presence of the Testator and of each other have hereunto subscribed our names as witnesses.

Dated at Salisbury this 20 day of March, A. D. 1819.

Gabriel Dutcher.

Thaddeus Root.
Lydia Anderson.
Joshua T. Jacobs.
Children:
I. Mary, born October 19, 1769; died 1818.
II Joshua, born December 16, 1770.
III. Sarah, born October 17, 1777; married _____ Dickson.
IV. Catherine, born July 2, 1774; married Elisha Deming, (his second wife.)
V. Lowrance, born August , 1776.
VI. John, born March 12, 1778.

Lowrance Dutcher, fifth child of Gabriel (5), (Johannes 4, Ruluff 3), was born August 1776; married Eunice Deming, born Jan. 21, 1793, died July 15, 1874. He died April 24, 1815. She married (2) Andrew Sardam.

Eunice Deming was daughter of Elisha Deming, born July 29, 1759, and Mary, his first wife; granddaughter of Dr. Elias Deming, of Goshen, Connecticut, and Hillsdale, New York, born Nov. 7, 1721, and Eunice Harris, his wife, whom he married April 7, 1757, at Goshen; great grand daughter of Benjamin Deming, born Jan. 20, 1684, of Wethersfield, and his wife Mary Wickham, whom he married Feb. 4, 1704 (6); great, great granddaughter of Jonathan Deming, born, 1639, died Jan. 8, 1700, of Wethersfield, and Elizabeth Gilbert, his wife; great great, great granddaughter of Hon. John Deming, born in England 1615, one of the founders of Connecticut, Deputy to the General Court, 1649-1661, one of the Patentees of Connecticut, named in the Royal Charter, 1662, and Honor Treat, his wife, who was the daughter of Hon. Richard Treat, born 1584, Deputy to the First General Court of Connecticut, 1637-1644, for Wethersfield, Assistant, 1657-1665, named in the Royal Charter as one of the Patentees of Connecticut, 1662, member of Gov. John Winthrop's Council, 1663-1665.

Only child of Lowrance and Eunice Dutcher:

Henry, born May 21, 1812. (Called Harry upon Salisbury records.)

Henry Dutcher, (Lowrance 6, Gabriel 5, Johannes 4, Ruluff 3), youngest child of Lowrance and Eunice (Deming) Dutcher, was born May 21, 1812, at Salisbury; married Sept. 3, 1833, Jane Mason, born July 4, 1816. She was daughter of Col Darius Mason, born Jan. 7, 1777, of Sheffield, Mass., and his wife Sarah Root, born Sept. 19, 1779; granddaughter of Peter Mason, born Aug. 1, 1752, and his wife Elisheba Farnham, born May 26, 1754, at Killingworth, Conn.; great granddaughter of Peter Mason, born Dec. 28, 1717, and his wife Margaret Fanning; great, great granddaughter of Captain Peter Mason, born Nov. 7, 1680, and Mary Hobart, his wife; great, great, great granddaughter of Captain Daniel Mason, born April , 1652, and his wife Rebecca Hobart, daughter of Rev. Peter Hobart, of Hingham, Mass.; great, great, great, great granddaughter of Major John Mason, commander-in-chief of the colonial forces during the Pequot War, 1637, and Deputy Governor of Connecticut, 1660-1670.

Sarah Root, above named, was daughter of Aaron Root, born March 21, 1750, and Sarah Bird, his wife (daughter of Capt. Joseph Bird and widow Sarah Eldridge); granddaughter of Col. Aaron Root, born Dec. 20, 1720, who served in the Revolution, and Rhoda King, his wife, born May 13, 1731, (daughter of Moses and Hester (Noble) King); great granddaughter of Ensign Joseph Root, born June 16, 1688, who was son of Thomas Root, born 1648, son of John Root, of Connecticut.

Hester Noble, above named, born June 6, 1710, was daughter of Matthew Noble and Hannah Dewey, born Feb. 21, 1672, and granddaughter of Mathew Noble, the emigrant. Hannah Dewey was the daughter of Cornet Thomas Dewey, born Feb. 16, 1640, and granddaughter of Thomas Dewey, the ancestor of the American family.

Henry and Jane Dutcher resided all their lives at Sheffield, in the house that was built for her the year of her marriage, by her father Col. Mason. On Sept. 3, 1893, they celebrated their sixtieth wedding anniversary by a family reunion. For over fifty years they were members of the Congregational Church, and were always active in religious and charitable work. Their lives of purity, noble self-sacrifice, and devotion to every trust reposed in them, will ever be held in most affectionate remembrance by their descendants. He died Nov. 30, 1894, in consequence of an accidental fall; she died of pneumonia, Jan. 12, 1901.

Children of Henry and Jane Dutcher:

I. CHARLES HENRY, born Aug. 21, 1835. (See record.)

II. Sarah Mason, born Oct. 9, 1842, married Theodore Curtis Wickwire. s. p.

III. Alfred Lowrance, born Dec. 20, 1852; married Matilda S. Drake. He was manager of the Brooklyn office of the Hanover Insurance Company. He died _____. They had one child:

Miriam, born _____, 1877; married April 23, 1901, Julian M. Pinkney, of New York City.

Charles Henry Dutcher, eldest child of Henry and Jane (Mason) Dutcher, (Henry 7, Lowrance 6, Gabriel 5, Johannes 4, Ruluff 3), was born at Sheffield, Mass., Aug. 21, 1835. He attended the public school and the academy in his native town, after which he went to Hartford, Conn., and engaged in mercantile business. He removed to New York City in 1855, and engaged for a time in the commission business. At the breaking out of the war in 1861, he enlisted in Company A, 13th N. Y. S. M. as private. His regiment was assigned to the command of Gen. B. F. Butler, and was stationed at first at Annapolis, Md., and was on duty there and elsewhere for several weeks. Mr. Dutcher continued with his regiment until his term of service expired. He returned home intending to re-enlist, but sickness in his family and other causes necessitated his remaining at home. In 1865 he formed a connection with the Continental Fire Insurance Company of New York, and served in various capacities without interruption, and at the present time is Secretary of the Brooklyn Department of the Company.

Mr. Dutcher has been an active worker in the Baptist denomination in Brooklyn for many years; was one of the organizers of the Baptist Home of Brooklyn and was its Secretary from April 13, 1875, to Nov. 13, 1883, and is now (1902) its President.

He was a constituent member of the Emanuel Baptist Church and has served as deacon since its organization. He was Superintendent of the Sunday School for many years. He is Treasurer of the Brooklyn Boys' Club, which he assisted in organizing· He is a member of the Veteran Association 13th Regiment, also of the Society of Old Brooklynites and other organizations. He married April 21, 1859, Amanda Story, daughter of Captain Henry and Eliza (Bond) Story. She was born June 4, 1839. He was a member of U. S. Grant Post No. 327, Department of New York, Grand Army of the Republic.

Children of Charles Henry and Amanda Dutcher:

I. Dora Harriet, born March 29, 1860; died Dec. 21, 1860.

II. Charles Mason, born Feb. 1, 1862; married Nov. 12, 1891, Helen Torrey Harris, daughter of Col. Frederick H. and Elizabeth (Torrey) Harris, President of American Insurance Company, Newark, N. J. He is accountant of the Greenwich Savings Bank of New York City. They had two children:

1. Frederick Harris, born Dec. 5, 1892.

2. Charles Mason, born Aug. 1, 1897; died Sept. 4, 1898.

III. Louise Edna, born Jan. 13, 1865; married Nov. 18, 1896, Arthur Manley Wickwire. He is a lawyer, and resides at St. Paul, Minn. They had two children:

1. Arthur Manley Wickwire, born Oct. 5, 1897; bapt. Nov. 11, 1898.

2. Charles Dutcher Wickwire, born April 19, 1899; bapt. June 17, 1900; died Jan. 7, 1901.

IV. Bessie Story, born Feb. 7, 1870; married April 21, 1898, David G. Sarles, of Brooklyn. He is manager of New York Woven Label Co. They have one child:

Kenneth Dutcher Sarles, born May 26, 1899.

V. William Hawley, born Feb. 7, 1870; married Nov. 17, 1897, Margaret Adna Young, born Sept 5, 1875, daughter of James Edward and Margaret Anna (McKee) Young. He is Secretary of Pratt & Lambert, Varnish Manufacturers.

VI. Theodore Shotwell, born Jan. 28, 1873.

VII. Edwin Brown, born April 10, 1880.

LINE OF GABRIEL DUTCHER, YOUNGEST SON AND EIGHTH CHILD OF ROELOFF ANE JANNETJI BRESSIE DUTCHER.

Gabriel Dutcher, eighth child of Roeloff and Jannetji (Bressie) De Duyster, was born July 15, 1720. He removed from Dutchess County, N. Y., to Salisbury, Conn., with his parents, where he spent the best years of his life in happiness and contentment. His brothers were settled around him and all remained in Salisbury until some time after their father's death. He inherited his portion of the estate, as appears by the following record:

"Whereas, we, Christopher Dutcher, of Canaan, and Johannes, Cornelius, Ruluff and Gabriel, of Salisbury, have all of us a share in the land lying in Salisbury formerly Wetauge, deceased, left to us, his children, excepting the orchard and the House Lot, a legacy in our said father's last will and testament bearing date Jan, 17, 1736, was given to *Gabriel*."

Executed July 24, 1758. In the meantime, Christopher died and Herty Dutcher, his widow, his sons, heirs of Christopher, signed with the rest.

The following item of interest appears on the Salisbury records:

SALISBURY, October 21, 1757.

Received by me, Gabriel Dutcher, of Salisbury, of Oliver Wolcott of Litchfield, sheriff of Litchfield County, four negroes. The one of said negroes is named Tom, aged about 50; another named Mary, a woman, and aged about 50; another named Zach, aged about 11; another named Adam, aged about 6 years, which said negroes were this day taken before ye sd. Wolcott by virtue of an execution granted out　*　*　*　in favor of Jeremiah Hogoboom of Claverack, against John Dutcher of Salisbury. Said execution demands £95-7-7, New York money, and said estate is taken from ye said John, which said estate I hereby promise well and safely to keep till ye tenth day of November next, and then to deliver ye said negroes to said Wolcott at ye public sign-post at Salisbury.

Gabriel Dutcher married, in Salisbury, Conn., Elizabette Knickerbacor (Knickerbocker), bap. in the Dutch Church at Kingston, N. Y., Jan. 7, 1722, daughter of Cornelius Knickerbacor and Jean Shut, son of Herman Jansen Knickerbocker, son of Johannes Van Bergen Knickerbocker.

"The name of Knickerbocker," says Gen. Viele in his history of this family (Harper's Magazine, 1876), "has become a generic term

by which are designated the descendants of the original Dutch settlers of the State of New York, and has here the same significance
as the word 'creole' in Louisiana (referring to the natives of the State
of Louisiana born of French or Spanish parents), which is applied to
those whose families date back to early occupation of that State by
the French. In more recent times 'Knickerbocker' has become a
favorite prefix to numerous products of industry and a popular name
for ships, steamers, hotels and companies of every description, until
the very origin of the word has been almost lost in its multitudinous
significations.

"In reality, this now universal patronymic belongs to one of
those ancient Dutch families who, as long ago as the seventeenth
century, were long proprietors in the fertile valley of the Mohawk
and upper Hudson, that section of the State having been selected for
occupancy by the early settlers of means and social position in preference to the uninviting region near the metropolis, which was left
to traders and market gardeners, the scanty soil offering no attrac-
tions, as it could only be cultivated in limited patches between the
rocky ridges.   *   *   *   *   *   *   *   *

"The early Dutch residents of Albany and its vicinity constituted
a kind of landed aristocracy, and, with their numerous retainers and
slaves, held a sort of feudal court in the grand mansions which may
still be found dotted here and there in the interior of the State.

"The family seat of the Knickerbockers at Schaghticoke is one
of the ancestral homes around whose hearthstones the associations of
bygone generations gather in the shadow of advancing times. The
spacious edifice is built in the quaint Flemish style of architecture,
with its deep pyramidally shaped roof like that of the venerable

THE OLD KNICKERBOCKER HOMESTEAD, SCHAGHTICOKE.

Dutch church that formerly stood in the center of State street in the city of Albany. * * The principal entrance is reached through an avenue of ancient trees, time-worn and scarred, that climb high above the roof, like watch-towers overlooking the plain. The vine-covered porch, with its hospitable seat on either side, welcomes the visitor, and the huge brass knocker, on the upper leaf of the old-fashioned oaken door, summons the cheerful host.

"Among the founders of the now prosperous Commonwealth of New York this family was conspicuous in the council and in the field. The head of the family in America was Herman Jansen Knickerbocker, son of Johannes Von Bergen Knickerbocker. He was born in Friesland, Holland, in the year 1648, entered the Dutch navy at an early age, and served under Van Tromp and De Ruyter during that period in the history of Holland which was so remarkable for its naval victories. He was severely wounded at the battle of Solebay, off the coast of England, where the Dutch ships engaged the combined English and French fleets. On his recovery he resigned his commission and came to America, where he soon after married Lysbeth Jane Bogart, daughter of Myndert Hermance Van De Bogart, the well known surgeon of the Dutch ship Endraaght, and subsequently commissary of Fort Orange. Van De Bogart was an eccentric and high-tempered individual. At one time, in a dispute with Piter Stuyvesant, the Director-General, while they were crossing the river, he attempted to throw the lusty Pieter overboard, and would have succeeded had he not been prevented. He died a violent death brought on by his ungovernable temper."

Referring to the later generations of the Knickerbocker family, Gen. Egbert L. Viele says:

"The time came at length when, after constant years of anxiety and watching, the quiet repose of peace settled over the valley of Schaghticoke (pronounced Skat-o-coke, said to be an Algonquin word signifying 'The Meeting of the Waters'), but this was soon rudely disturbed by the gathering clouds that presaged the struggle of the colonies with Great Britain. The Dutch settlers had loyally served the States General and their authorized agents, and had afterwards been equally true to the Duke of York and to the British sovereign. The several generations of the Knickerbocker family, as they came upon the active stage of life, took their place and performed their part in current affairs. Colonel Johannes Knickerbocker served in various expeditions against the hostile Indian tribes; was afterwards attached to the staff of Lord Howe in the attack on Ticonderoga in 1758. He was commissioned a colonel in the Revolutionary Army, Oct. 20, 1775, raised a regiment in Schaighticoke, and was severely wounded at the battle of Saratoga. He was also a member of the State Legislature in 1792."

Mrs. Lydia Sigourney, whose classic poems are among the richest treasures of American History, visited the old Knickerbocker mansion and wrote the following lines:

"O vale of peace! O haunt serene!
    O hill encircled shades!
No footsteps rude, or fiery neigh
    Of iron steed o'er graded way
    Your Sylvan steep invades.

"The red-browed Indian's planted name
    Your blended waters bore,
Though they who erst that baptism gave
    Beneath oblivion's blackening wave
    Have sunk to rise no more.

" Here, clad in ancient honor, dwelt
    The Knickerbocker race,
And wisely ruled in hall and bower,
    And held their old memorial power
    With firm and honest grace.

" There gatherings grand of social joy
    The ancestral mansions knew;
While roof and rafter shook with mirth,
    And hospitality had birth,
    Which still is warm and true.

"So may the Knickerbocker line
    Their prosperous harvest sow,
Nor ever lack a noble heir
    Their dynasty and name to bear
    While mingling waters flow."

Referring to the marriages between the Knickerbocker and other well-known families of New York State, Gen. Viele says:

" As a matter of course these early settlers depended greatly upon each other; there was ever present a common danger to bind them together, while the social necessities of life held them in firm bonds of friendship. As a natural result, intermarriages between the families soon added the still stronger ties of consanguinity, and at the present time there is scarcely an individual for many miles around that is not in some way related to all the others.

Life at Schaghticoke was for many years like an armed reconnoissance. The lurking savage was always on the lookout for a victim, and the subtle Canadian ever conspiring for an attack. Each and all were compelled to be constantly on the alert. In the midst of

COLONEL JOHANNES KNICKERBOCKER AND HIS WIFE.—[FROM A PAINTING IN THE EAST ROOM.]

their troubles the settlers did not for a moment lose sight of their religious duties. A Dutch Reformed church was erected under the auspices of the Classis of Amsterdam. Over this the venerable Dominie Vanschooten ministered. The rude place of worship originally built was soon replaced by a more imposing edifice. This quaint building was sixty by forty feet, with low side walls and a high-pitched mansard roof, and turret surmounted by weathercock over the southern gable. The services of the church were, of course, in the Dutch language, and the old time-stained Bible with brass corners and huge brass clasps, then in use, is now an heirloom reverently preserved in the Knickerbocker mansion."

Munsell's Annals of Albany says of this family of Knickerbockers: Herman Jansen Knickerbocker was the son of Johannes Van Berghen and his wife Johannes, daughter of Rutger Van Marnix, Lord of Boteclear. In his will, January 7, 1701, he mentions six children, baptised in the Reformed Dutch church at Albany.

Cornelis, bap. Sept. 2, 1688, died soon.

Cornelis, again, bap. Jan. 6, 1692.

Cornelia, bap. July 20, 1695.

Evert, bap. Sept. 8, 1699.

Pieter, bap. April 19, ——.

Johannes and Laurens are mentioned in his will, but the dates of baptism are not given, and the name of Cornelis, which appears among his children, is not mentioned in this will.

Cornelius Knickerbocker, or Knickerbacor, as it appears on the Connecticut records, son of Herman Jansen Knickerbacker, was baptised Jan. 6, 1692, at Albany, and soon after he attained his majority moved to Litchfield, Conn. The History of Litchfield

County states that "The Knickerbocker family came into town (Salisbury) soon after White and others. John (Johannes) Knickerbacor occupied that Knickerbacor grant. Cornelius, his brother, settled at Furnace Village about the same time. Cornelius Knickerbacor's was for some time the only white family in that section of the town." He afterward removed to Sharon, Conn.

Cornelius Knickerbacor married Johannes Shut and had, among other children, a daughter Elizabeth, who was married to Gabriel Dutcher, December, 1743.

Gabriel Dutcher returned to Dutchess County after 1759, and probably resided there among his wife's friends until her death at Dover Plains, N. Y., April 23, 1793, when he removed to Cherry Valley, N. Y., and spent the remainder of his days with his son John. His wife was buried in the old graveyard at Dover Plains, and the simple tombstone contains the following inscription:

Elizabeth, Wife of Gabriel Dutcher, died April 23, 1793, Æ 73.

Gabriel Dutcher, by his wife Elizabeth (Knickerbacor) Dutcher, had issue:

    I. *Benjamin*, bap. in the Germantown Church, Columbus Co., Jan. 29, 1744.

    II. Cornelius, bap. in the Germantown Church, May 24, 1746.

    III. *Christoffell*, bap. in the Germantown Church, Jan. 3, 1748.

    IV. Catharine, born Sept. 18, 1749.

        Between the births of Catharine and John there were other children born, but their baptisms do not appear on the records of the Germantown Church and they have not been found elsewhere.

    V. *John*, born Jan. 5, 1759.

In Memory of
Elizabeth the wife of
Gabril Dutcher, who
Died April 23^d 1793
in the 73^d year of her
age.

On God's Almighty name I call'd,
And thus to him I pray'd;
Lord I befeech thee fave my foul
With forrows quite difmay'd.

After the death of Gabriel Dutcher, the father, the estate at Salisbury was divided up and the children soon became scattered, and only the ancient landmarks are left as a reminder of the Dutch settlement in this locality.

Benjamin, the eldest child, removed to Dutchess County, N. Y., and married there. He subsequently moved to Washington County, N. Y., and finally to Shaftsbury, Vt., where he died. The next of his descendants appears under the head of "Benjamin Dutcher and His Descendants," after that of John, who was the youngest son of Gabriel.

Of Cornelius, the second child, little is known, and his descendants are probably scattered in different parts of the country.

Christoffel or Christopher Dutcher, whose baptism is found on the records of the Germantown Church as May 24, 1746, appears to have been a man of considerable push and energy. He took advantage of the division of the estate belonging to the Livingston Manor, not long after the Manor ceased to exist, and bought a large tract of land extending from the top of Chestnut Ridge at Dover Plains, in Dutchess County, N. Y., to the Ten Mile River. He not only carried on an extensive farm, but he erected a mill on Ten Mile River where he ground the wheat and corn for his neighbors for miles around. He married Mary Belden, daughter of Silas Belden, a native of Wethersfield, Conn., and the founder of the Belden family of Dutchess County, N. Y. They had a son, Lawrence Dutcher, who married Jane Nasse, and had a son, Belden Dutcher, born Aug. 9, 1793. The latter married Maria Hurd and had Egbert, married Maria Soule, who were the parents of Mary Ellen Dutcher, who married for her second husband Richard P. Ketcham.

LINE OF JOHN DUTCHER, YOUNGEST SON OF GABRIEL AND ELIZABETH (KNICKERBOCKER) DUTCHER.

John Dutcher, youngest son of Gabriel and Elizabeth (Knickerbacor) Dutcher, was born at Salisbury, Conn., Jan. 5th, 1759, died Dec. 2nd, 1848. He moved to Dover, Dutchess Co., N. Y., and thence to Cherry Valley, Otsego County, N. Y. He married Sylvia Beardsley, May 17th, 1779, daughter of Johiel, son of John (2), son of John (1), son of Joseph, son of William, the ancestor. She was born October 10, 1763, died January 14th, 1844.

William Beardsley, the ancestor of the Beardsley family of Stratford, Conn., came from England in 1635 in the ship *Planter* at the age of 30, with his wife Mary, daughter Mary, sons John and Joseph. Tradition says he was a native of Stratford on Avon, the home of Shakespeare, and that he gave the name Stratford to the plantation in Connecticut where he settled, and that one of his descendents who moved to Livingston County, N. Y., gave the name to the place where he settled, Avon, in honor of the river from whence his ancestor came. William Beardsley emigrated with Rev. Adam Blackeman from St. Albans, England, was at Hadley, Mass., until 1638, removing thence to Hartford, Conn., and was one of the original settlers of Stratford. He was seven times elected Deputy to the General Court of Connecticut. He died at the age of 56 years. In his will he says, "All my daughters that are now married, I give ten pounds apiece." He had nine children of whom Joseph was the third.

Joseph Beardsley, third child of William and Mary (——) Beardsley, was born in England, came with his parents to America and lived in Stratford. His father left him half of his estate, after other bequests, provided he should leave the life of a seaman and take care of his mother. He complied so far as to secure the property which he exchanged July 31, 1684 (he being then of Brookhaven, L. I.), with Andrew Gibb " All his possessions in Stratford, for Mr. Gibb's homestead in Brookhaven." He married Abigail ———, and had nine children of whom John (1) was the second.

John Beardsley (1) son of Joseph and Abagail (———) Beardsley, was born Nov. 4th, 1668. He was a blacksmith. In his will dated Nov. 11th, 1732, he mentions his wife Abigail and five sons. His will is recorded in Fairfield, Conn. He gave land in Unity and Great Neck to his son Andrew. To Johiel he said, " I give my shop and all my working tools for the carrying on of my trade, and my cart and my wheels, and all my lot and orchard at Walnut-tree Hill." He married Abigail Wakelyn and had six children, of whom John (2) was the fifth.

John Beardsley (2), son of John (1) and Abigail (Wakelyn) Beardsley, was born March 9, 1701. He married Keziah Wheeler, Dec. 29, 1725. He received from his father " for paternal love" 36 acres of land on lower White Hills. They had issue Johiel.

Johiel Beardsley, fifth son of John (2) and Keziah (Wheeler) Beardsley, was born Feb. 9th, 1733. He married Hannah Griffin and had among other children a daughter, Sylvia, who was married to John Dutcher.

John Dutcher by his wife, Sylvia (Beardsley) Dutcher had issue:

I. Elizabeth, born May 18th, 1780, died June 8th, 1780.

II. *Christopher*, born April 25th, 1781, died April 23d, 1845, married Martha Sloan.

III. Gabriel, born May 5th, 1783, married Peggie McKillip, died May 21st, 1849, had three sons, Daniel, Dwight and Davis.

IV. Hannah, born April 26, 1785, married Mr. Fitch and afterwards Simon Gray, died Jan. 10, 1862.

V. Johiel, born April 24, 1787, died Jan. 14, 1822, single.

VI. Sylvia, born March 2, 1789, married Wm. Goodell, died Nov. 5, 1865.

VII. Sally, born July 31, 1791, married Wm. Knapp, died March 21, 1842.

VIII. *Parcefor Carr*, born Jan. 3, 1794, died Feb. 18, 1867, married Johanna Low Frink, Dec. 31, 1821; born July 2, 1802, died Sept. 7, 1881.

IX. Mary, born March 2, 1796, married John McKillip, died Feb. 16, 1882.

X. John, born Dec. 1, 1797, died March 22, 1859.

XI. Keziah, born March 14, 1800, married Benjamin Davis, died Oct. 4, 1878.

XII. Dr. Joseph N., born Sept. 9, 1802, married Louisa Spafford, died 1873.

XIII. Deborah White, born August 15, 1804, married Wm. Davis, died Oct. 24, 1868.

CHRISTOPHER DUTCHER, eldest son of John and Sylvia (Beardsley) Dutcher, born April 25, 1781, died April 23, 1845, married Martha Sloan, June 2, 1803, who was born May 3, 1784, died Jan. 3, 1875. They had issue: Sylvia, John and Christopher.

Children:

I. Sylvia Dutcher was born June 3, 1804, died April 26, 1884. She was married March 14, 1822, to Peter Gilchrist, of Springfield, N. Y. Second husband was Lewis Whipple, whom she married in

1840. The seven children of Sylvia Dutcher and Peter Gilchrist are as follows:

I. Martha Gilchrist, born April 10, 1823, died May 30, 1871. Married twice; first in 1839, to James Vibbard, who died in 1840. September 27, 1842, she married Gershom Shaul. Issue, five children: Sylvia, M. Libbie, Jennie, Squire Gilchrist, P. Lewis.

1. Sylvia Shaul, eldest child of Martha Gilchrist Shaul, born Aug. 21, 1843, married John T. Alwaise, Oct. 10, 1867, residence 158 W. 130 St., New York City.

2. M. Libbie Shaul, second child of Martha Gilchrist Shaul, born July 5, 1846, married Robert Lay Walrath, Feb. 10, 1870. Resides East Springfield, N. Y. Issue: John Jacob, Sylvia Elizabeth, Myra Loxea, Robert Homer.

John Jacob Walrath, born Nov, 26, 1870, married Florence L. Young, Dec. 12, 1894, and have issue: Louisa Elizabeth, born Feb. 15, 1898, Robert Young, born May 25, 1900, and Dorothy Eleanor, born Aug. 11, 1901. Residence East Springfield, N. Y.

Sylvia Elizabeth Walrath, born June 23, 1876, married Dr. Phillip S. Young, June 7, 1899. Residence East Springfield, N. Y.

Myra Loxea Walrath, born June 9, 1879, died Dec. 23, 1881.

Robert Homer Walrath, born Nov. 21, 1884.

3. Jennie Shaul, third child of Martha Gilchrist Shaul, born May 10, 1848, married June 4, 1873, John J. Lawrence. Resides 598 E. 140 St., New York City. Their children are:

R. Warren Lawrence, born May 8, 1874, married Nellie Logan Lawson Oct. 18, 1899. Residence 598 East 140 St., New York City.

Clinton Edward Lawrencc, born April 16, 1880.

John Jacob Lawrence, born Nov. 14, 1881.

4. Squire Gilchrist Shaul, fourth child of Martha Gilchrist Shaul, born June 25, 1850, married Oct. 4, 1871 Emma Wilcox of North Litchfield, N. Y. Residence North Bridgewater, N. Y. Their children are:

Charles W. Shaul, born Jan. 19, 1873, married Alice M. Carpenter, Jan. 10, 1900. Residence Cassville, N. Y. Have one child, Herman Edward, born Feb. 10, 1901.

Martha H. Shaul, born May 4, 1874, married Edward A. Miller of Clinton N. Y., June 1, 1899; they have one child, Bertha Louise, born August 28, 1901.

Frederich G. Shaul, born March 10, 1878, married Louise M. Healey of Gretna, La., June 26, 1901. Residence 305 Central Ave. West Hoboken, N. Y.

5. P. Lewis Shaul, born 1856, died 1862.

II. Mary Gilchrist was born April 15, 1824, twice married, first June 6, 1840, to Johnson Whipple (one child, Louise M.), again in December, 1861, to Felix M. Rice (one child, Franklin Sheldon). Her present home is E. Springfield. By her first husband she had Louisc M. Whipple, born February 12, 1842, died December 16, 1893, married Sheldon A. Young, October 17, 1866. By her second marriage she had Franklin Sheldon Rice, born October 3, 1866, died August 9, 1868.

III. Christopher Gilchrist, born March 30, 1825, died July 7, 1893. Married Melissa Harwick, November 23, 1854 (four children, Louis, Annie, died young, Kittie and Ernest). Kittie married Arthur Northrup, residence, Cullen, N. Y. Ernest married Lillie ——, one child, Marian.

IV. Jane A. Gilchrist, born January 1st, 1827, married John Scollard, January 18, 1871. No children. Residence, E. Springfield, N. Y.

V. Daniel Gilchrist, born November 21, 1828, married Hannah E. Walrath, January 2, 1866 (four children, Louise Walrath, Martha Irene, Evander Daniel and Addie Loxea). Residence of Daniel Gilchrist, E. Springfield, N. Y. Issue:

1. Louise Walrath Gilchrist, born Dec. 10, 1868.

2. Martha (Mattie) Irene Gilchrist, born May 16, 1871, died in Nebraska, March 25, 1891.

3. Daniel Evander Gilchrist, born July 27, 1876.

4. Addie Loxea Gilchrist, born June 13, 1878, married Edwin H. Marks, Dec. 18, 1901. Residence Johnstown, N. Y.

VI. Eliza Gilchrist, born Feb. 28, 1832, married Evander W. Barnum, February 23, 1860. Residence, Union, Cass County, Nebraska. They had issue:

1. Thomas G. Barnum, born Mar. 28, 1861, married November 8, 1883, Hattie A. Pollard (one child, Vernie P.), born Nov. 24, 1884. Residence, Union, Cass Co., Nebraska.

VII. Margaret A. Gilchrist, born August 1, 1834, died

February 28, 1896. Married Dexter J. Matteson, Jan. 16, 1861. Issue:

1. Evander W. Matteson, born Dec. 9, 1872, died Nov. 17, 1894.

JOHN DUTCHER, second child and eldest son of Christopher and Martha Sloan Dutcher, born Nov. 15, 1807, died Nov. 4, 1875, married Laura Burlingame, Jan. 30, 1830, who was born June 28, 1811, died April 23, 1844. Children: Squire, Keziah, Louisa, Mary, Monroe and John.

Squire Dutcher, born Oct. 31, 1830, married Jennie Brewster. Children: Byram, De Forrest.

Keziah Dutcher, born Jan. 25, 1832, married Daniel Mason. Children: Alma, Edric, Laura, Linus.

Louisa Dutcher, born July 17, 1833, married Adrial Parshall. Children: John Adelbert, Belle and Claud Parshall. John Adelbert married Olive Clark. Belle married Curtis Barnum. Claud married Lena Snedicker.

Mary Dutcher, born Jan. 21, 1837, married Horace Pierce. Children: Arthur W., Laura.

Monroe Dutcher, born Oct. 7, 1839, married Jennie Gates. No children.

John Dutcher, Jr., born April 2, 1844, married Eliza Phillips. No children. Married second wife Aug. 7, 1896, Elizabeth Skinion, born May 1, 1864.

CHRISTOPHER DUTCHER, youngest son of Christopher and Martha Sloan Dutcher, was born July 15, 1815, died September 14, 1893, married Roxie Baird, October 11, 1838, who died April 4, 1883. They had issue Jerome W., Lewis W., Martha E., Esther M.

I. Jerome W., born August 1, 1839, died July 16, 1901. He married Gertrude M. Burlingame, February 4, 1858. They had issue:

Laura Dutcher, born March 20, 1859.

Christopher Dutcher, born April 11, 1861.

Anna Dutcher, born June 8, 1863, died July 7, 1901.

Thomas B. Dutcher, born Aug. 4, 1864.

William J. Dutcher, born September 5, 1871.

II. Lewis W., born August 6, 1843, married Emma D. Moone, September 28, 1864, at Hartwick Seminary, where they now (1902) reside. She was born Dec. 29, 1839. They had issue born at E. Springfield:

Lewis Belden, born Nov. 23, 1865, married Dec. 30, 1894, to Grace M. Strail, Schoharie Co. No children. He is a Lutheran clergyman. His first charge was Freysbush, Montgomery Co., N. Y., from April, 1893, to April, 1899. His present charge is Stone Arabia, since 1899. He was graduated from Hartwick Seminary in 1891.

Arthur Winfield, born Dec. 2, 1867, died July 27, 1899.

Fred Christopher, born Aug. 26, 1869, married Hannah Judkins, of Westford, March 27, 1899. They had issue, Arthur W., born May 7, 1901. Fred C. is a farmer and resides at Hartwick Seminary.

The following children born at Hartwick Seminary:

Emma Louise, born August 30, 1873, married Alfred Churchill Clark, Nov. 8, 1898. Residence California.

Martha Esther, born Feb. 19, 1876, died Feb, 9, 1879.

Ralph Lee, born April 16, 1877, died Aug. 10, 1877.

III. Martha E., born April 18, 1850, married Theodore L. Grout, February 19, 1892, died July 17, 1895. No issue.

IV. Esther M., born May 10, 1853, married Theodore L. Grout, October 8, 1873, died December 26, 1883. They had issue:

    Everett T., born October 17, 1879.

    Edwin D., born November 4, 1882.

MARY DUTCHER, ninth child of John and Sylvia (Beardsley) Dutcher, born March 2, 1796, died February 16, 1882, married April, 1821, to John McKillip, born 1790, died December 24, 1845. Children:

    Daniel Beardsley, born June, 1822, died Oct. 17, 1900.

    Deborah Elizabeth, born Sept, 1825, died Feb. 26, 1867.

    Joseph Gabriel, born November, 1828.

    John Archibald, born 1834, drowned July 22, 1865.

KEZIA DUTCHER, eleventh child of John and Sylvia (Beardsley) Dutcher, born at Cherry Valley, March 14, 1800, died October 4, 1878, married April 28, 1822, Benjamin Davis, born at Burlington, N. J., October 5, 1795, died March 25, 1860. Children:

    Hannah Elizabeth, born Dec. 16, 1825.

    William Alonzo, born June 16, 1828; died May 21, 1843.

    Mary Jane, born June 22, 1831, died Oct. 30, 1898, married Amos Latimer Swan, Nov. 12, 1873, who died Sept. 4, 1881. No children.

    Harriet Keziah, born Sept. 3, 1833, died May 20, 1843.

    Benjamin Bruce, born Feb. 12, 1836, died Nov. 1, 1880, married December 25, 1872, Mrs. Sophia Davidson.

    Jos. Warren, born Oct. 20, 1837, died Aug. 19, 1883, married April 28, 1880, Sarah A. Nellis.

    Catharine Sylvia, born Dec. 19, 1841, married Nov. 12,

PARCEFOR C. DUTCHER.

JOHANNA LOW DUTCHER.

MRS. AGNES A. ROOT NEE DUTCHER.

MISS HARRIET E. DUTCHER.

1873, Almond Brown, who died March 7, 1893. Children:

Benjamin Davis Brown, born Aug. 29, 1874.

Edith Juan Brown, born April 12, 1876.

Mary Elizabeth Brown, born Feb. 2, 1879.

Sylvia Brown, born March 30, 1884.

DEBORAH WHITE DUTCHER, thirteenth child of John and Sylvia (Beardsley) Dutcher, born Aug. 15, 1804, died Oct. 24, 1868, was married Sept. 25, 1825, to William Davis, born April 6, 1801, died July 22, 1876. Their children are:

I. Joseph Dutcher Davis, born Sept. 9, 1827, died Sept. 19, 1865, married Aug. 5, 1850, Martha L. Howe.

II. William Kirby Davis, born Jan. 31, 1829, died Feb. 25, 1887, married Aug. 12, 1855, Anna B. Nostine.

III. Lewis Benjamin Davis, born Oct. 26, 1830, died June 13, 1901.

IV. John Leonard Davis, born Nov. 3, 1834, died Aug. 14, 1900, married Dec. 20, 1856, Louisa Hanenstein.

V. Mary Beardsley Davis, born Feb. 3, 1837, died Dec. 24, 1843.

VI. Hannah Ann Davis, born Jan. 21, 1840, married Sept. 7, 1865, Trustman B. Totten.

Parcefor Carr Dutcher, eighth child of John and Sylvia (Beardsley) Dutcher, was born January 3, 1794, at Cherry Valley, Otsego County, New York. He died February 18, 1867. He purchased a farm in Springfield, in the same county, on which he resided until 1846, when he removed to Seneca, Ontario County, New York.

His whole life was spent in a quiet way in the cultivation of his farm with no desire for public life. He and his wife were members of the Presbyterian Church in which they were earnest and active workers.

He married, Dec. 31, 1821, Johanna Low Frink, born July 2, 1802, died September 7, 1881, while on a visit at Roseboom, Otsego County, New York, within a mile of the place where she was born.

She was a daughter of Stephen Frink of Connecticut, a descendent probably in the fifth generation of Lieutenant John Frink of Stonington.

Lieutenant John Frink was an early settler of Stonington, Conn. In the contract for building the new meeting-house, October, 1680, John Frink of Stonington and Edward De Wolf of Lynn were called in to view the work and arbitrate between the builders and people. He was formerly of Roxbury, Mass.

In October, 1696, Lieutenant Thomas Liffingwill of Norwich and Sergeant John Frink of Stonington, moved the General Court "that they, with the rest of the English volunteers in former wars, might have a plantation granted to them." A tract of land six miles square was granted in answer to their request, "to be taken up out of some of the conquered land," its bounds prescribed and settlement regulated by persons appointed by the court. * * A large part of the tract thus granted is now comprised in the town of Voluntown, Windham County.

July 1, 1701, the grantees met in Stonington to make arrangements for survey and appropriation. Richard Bushnell was chosen clerk of the company, and desired to make out a list of names of volunteers and also to make entry of such votes as should be passed. Thomas Liffingwill, James Avery, *John Frink*, and Richard Smith were chosen as committee "to pass all that should offer themselves as volunteers."

STEPHEN FRINK

The Frinks settled probably in Pomfret and Sterling, Windham County, as the name appears quite frequently on the records. From the foregoing record it is evident that Lieutenant John Frink served in the French and Indian War.

That the Frinks were of an excellent family is shown in the fact that they were united by marriage to the best families in New London County. In "Old Houses of the Antient Town of Norwich" by Mary E. Perkins, page 40, is the following:

"Col. Zedekiah Huntington, born in Norwich, 1696, married 1719, Hannah Frink, whom we believe to be a daughter of Samuel and Hannah (Miner) Frink of Stonington, Conn."

Capt. Nathan Frink, probably son or grandson of Lieut. John Frink, was one of the most brilliant lawyers in Windham County. He was for some years King Attorney for the County, and stood very high in the community.

Stephen Frink, born January 18, 1777, died January 11, 1860, the father of Johanna Low Frink (wife of Parcefor Carr Dutcher), married in 1796, Ann Low, daughter of Capt. Peter Low.

Capt. Peter Low, born January 4, 1750, died April 10, 1820, was the son of Cornelius Low, who in 1728, had a grant of 230 acres of land in Branchville, Somerset County, N. J. He served with honor in the war of the Revolution. He entered the army as private in Capt. Ten Eyck's Company, promoted First Lieutenant Capt. Styles Company, July 5, 1776, First Lieutenant Col. Thompson's Battalion, "Detached Militia," July 18, 1776, also First Lieutenant Continental Army, "New Jersey Line," and was afterwards promoted Captain. He was in many important engagements and commanded a company at the Battle of Monmouth. He resided at

North Branch, Somerset County, N. J., and in 1788 moved to Cherry Valley, Otsego County, New York. He married, February 26, 1778, Johanna Ten Eyck, born October 30, 1751, died July 17, 1834, daughter of Mattys (or Matthew Ten Eyck), son of Jacob, son of Matthew, son of Conradt Ten Eyck.

Johanna Low's first husband was Peter Sutphin, who died in 1874, and by whom she had two children, Peter, born December 19, 1770, and Eleanor, born June 9, 1773.

Conraedt Ten Eyck, the ancestor, emigrated from Amsterdam, Holland, to America, in 1650, and located in New York City, where he owned what is now called Coenties Slip. He died in New York City, and his remains are supposed to have been interred beneath the old Dutch Reformed Church that stood on Nassau Street, the present site of the New York Mutual Life Insurance Company. He married Maria Boele, who came with him from Holland, and by whom he had eleven children, among whom was *Matthys*.

Matthys Ten Eyck, youngest child of Conraedt and Maria (Boele) Ten Eyck, was born in New York City, May 18, 1658. At an early age he removed to Old Hurley, Ulster County, N. Y., where he engaged in farming and, to some extent, in the transportation business on the Hudson river. He was a man of influence and prominence; was assessor of the town 1724, supervisor 1725, and filled an important place in the community. He was one of the founders of the Reformed Church of Hurley. He died in 1741, and a humble stone in the burying ground at Hurley village marks his resting place. He married Jannikin, daughter of Aldert Roosa, another pioneer settler of Hurley, October 22, 1679, and had Albert, Andries, Conraedt, Jacob, Abraham, Wyntie, Mariete, Grietie, Ragdt.

ANN LOW FRINK

Jacob Ten Eyck, son of Matthys, was born in Hurley, 1693. On October 20, 1725, he received by deed from his father, for the consideration of five hundred pounds current money, five hundred acres of land on the northerly side of the North Branch of the Raritan river, N. J. He took up his residence on the tract and added considerable to it. He erected on it a one and a half story house of the old Dutch style. He married Jemima Van Nest, daughter of Jerome Van Nest, of Somerville, N. J., and had issue, Jacob, Matthew (or Matthys), Coenrad, Peter, Cattren, Jaen, Hannah. He died in 1753, willing his property to his son Jacob.

Matthys, or Matthew Ten Eyck, son of Jacob, was born in New Jersey. He married Nellie Tunison and had a daughter, Johannah, born October 30, 1751, died July 17, 1834, who was married to Capt. Peter Low, born January 4, 1750, died April 10, 1820, whose daughter, Ann Low, born November 27, 1778, was the wife of Stephen Frink, born January 18, 1777, married at Cherry Valley in 1796, whose daughter, Johanna Low Frink, was married to Parcefor Carr Dutcher, December 31.1821.

WILL OF MATTHIAS TEN EYCK, OF BRIDGEWATER, SOMERSET CO., N. J.

Date, September 29, 1783. Yeoman [Liber N, Folio 216].

Wife: Nellie.

Sons: Andries, Ten Eyck.

Nellie Griggs to have maintainance as long as she remains a single woman.

Daughters: Sarah, wife of Garret Tunison; Rebecca; Arinte, wife of John Wood; Nellie, wife of Gerrebrant Claoson, were children of Cornelius Williamson, deceased.

Johanna, wife of Peter Low. (She was the widow of Peter Sutphin.)

Jean, wife of Peter Davis.

Phebe, wife of Simon Probasca.

Grand-daughter: Cornelia, daughter of son Cornelius Ten Eyck, late dec'd.

Exec.: Sons-in-law Peter Davis, Peter Low, George Van Nest, son of Abraham and Andries Van Nidelswarts.

Witnesses: John King and Jacob Ten Eyck.

Probate, May 19, 1784.

The children of Parcefor Carr Dutcher and his wife Johannah Low (Frink) Dutcher were:

I. ANDREW DUTCHER, born August 29, 1822; married, Dec. 31, 1846, Harriet Martin Jenks. She died July 25, 1860. He married 2nd, Oct. 2, 1862, Marion Colton Holton.

II. SILAS B. DUTCHER, born July 12, 1829; married, February 10, 1859, Rebecca J. Alwaise.

III. Agnes Ann Dutcher, born April 2, 1836; married, Sept. 22, 1857, Edward Root.

IV. Harriet Elizabeth Dutcher, born Nov. 2, 1847; died Feb. 25, 1897.

Andrew Dutcher, eldest son of Parcefor C. and Johanna Low (Frink) Dutcher, was born on August 29, 1822, at East Springfield, Otsego County, New York. He was educated in the public and private schools of Otsego County, New York. In the intervals of attending school, he worked on his father's farm, and after finishing his education he continued for some years to work on the farm in summer, while teaching school in winter. Thus he was engaged until 1844, when he went to Ontario, LaGrange County, Indiana,

Andrew Dutcher

and began the study of law. He was admitted to the bar at Fort Wayne, Indiana, in August 1845, and at once began the practice of the profession. In 1847 he was elected Prosecuting Attorney for LaGrange County for three years and served that term, but on account of ill-health, declined a re-election. His health having become much impaired by climatic influences, he decided to leave Indiana, which he did in 1851, and removed to Trenton, New Jersey, where he remained until 1868, when he removed to Elizabeth, New Jersey, and finally in 1876, he settled in New York, in which city he has practiced law since 1868.

While in Trenton, Mr. Dutcher was a member of the School Board and of the City Council, City Attorney and Captain of a Military Company. He was a member of the State Assembly in 1856-57 and in the latter year was Speaker of the House. From 1856 to his resignation in 1865, he was Law Reporter for the Supreme Court of New Jersey and published five volumes of reports. From 1862 to 1869 he was Clerk of the United States Circuit Court of New Jersey. In Elizabeth, he was City Attorney, and held other municipal offices, and in 1872 was a member of the Legislature from Union County. Mr. Dutcher was a practitioner in all the Courts of New Jersey, in both civil and criminal cases.

In 1861 he was associated with the United States District Attorney in the trial of Jackalow for murder committed on Long Island Sound, the chief issue being whether the Federal Government or the Government of New York and Connecticut had jurisdiction over those waters. He had charge of the legal questions arising in the case and argued earnestly in favor of the jurisdiction of the Federal Government. The Court at first expressed an adverse opinion, but finally sustained Mr. Dutcher's views, and the prisoner was convicted.

In 1876, Mr. Dutcher was counsel for the property owners in the great case concerning assessments for street improvements in Elizabeth and argued the case in the New Jersey Court of Error and Appeals. That Court invalidated the assessments according to Mr. Dutcher's contentions, and the bankruptcy of the city followed. By this decision was overruled a previous decision of the Court in a case in which the same legal questions were involved.

In New York, Mr. Dutcher has not practiced in criminal cases, but has devoted himself to the practice of civil law and real estate, corporation and patent law in particular. In late years he has given up litigated cases and confined his attention to office business, the management and settlement of estates and services for corporations. He is counsel for several corporations and is frequently consulted as an authority on corporation law. He makes his home with his nephew, De Witt P. Dutcher, at 444 79th St., Brooklyn, N. Y.

Mr. Dutcher prepared his cases with extreme care; he saw quickly the strong points of his case; he was a sagacious examiner of witnesses and presented his evidence and the legal points with great force and clearness. His fairness and correctness in quoting precedents commanded the confidence of the higher courts and he was always listened to with respect in cases on appeal. He was a popular as well as forcible and convincing speaker, and his services were in demand in every important political campaign, but duty to his clients and the large volume of legal business prevented him from giving much attention to politics.

Andrew Dutcher, on December 31, 1846, married Harriet Martin Jenks, born August 7, 1824, died July 25, 1860; he subsequently married October 2, 1862, Marion Cotton Holton, born

November 12, 1842, and died February 29, 1884. By his first marriage, he had issue:

Harriet Jane, born December 29, 1851.

Alfred Carr, born October 12, 1855, married October 1, 1896, Adelia Tice. He has been for the past twenty years in the service of the Federal Government and is now connected with the Surveyors Department of the N. Y. Customs.

Andrew Belden, born January 6, 1858, died July 22, 1876.

By his second marriage, he had issue:

Marion Holton, born July 7, 1867, married February 11, 1890, Edward Yeomans, and died April 1, 1890.

Silas B. Dutcher, second child of Parcefor Carr and Johannah Low (Frink) Dutcher was born July 12, 1829, on his father's farm on the shore of Otsego Lake in the town of Springfield, Otsego County, N. Y. He attended the public schools near his father's farm, summer and winter, from the age of four until the age of seven years. After that he had a little more schooling in the winter season and one term at Cazenovia Seminary. He began teaching school winters at the age of sixteen and taught every winter until he was twenty-two, working on his father's farm during the balance of each year. In the fall of 1851, owing to a temporary loss of his voice which prevented him from teaching, he found employment at railroad construction and soon became a station agent and subsequently a conductor, and for more than than three years was employed on the railway from Elmira to Niagara Falls, New York. He then went to New York City and entered mercantile business, to which he devoted his energies from 1855 to 1868. During this time he passed through the panics of 1857 and 1860 without severe misfortune. In 1868 he was appointed Supervisor of Internal Revenue, a position which he at first declined, but was urged to accept by William Orton and other friends. Against his own judgment, and, as events proved, greatly to the detriment of his financial interests, he took the office. He was unable to give attention to business, his partner was not equal to its management, and he soon discovered that all he had accumulated by twelve years of hard work was scattered and gone, and he was obliged to sell the real estate he owned to meet his liabilities.

Even as a boy he had been more or less interested in politics. His grandfather was a Democrat and Silas was often called upon to read his Democratic newspaper to him; his father was a Whig and the result was that he had opportunity to learn something of the claims of both parties at an early age. Before he was twenty-one, he became interested in the question of freedom or the extension of slavery in the territories, the most vital question of that day, and while yet little more than a boy, in 1848, did some effective campaign speaking for General Taylor.

When he went to New York, Mr. Dutcher resolved to have nothing to do with active politics, but the breaking up of a Republican meeting in the Bleecker Building in the Ninth Ward brought him out most decisively and he was quite active politically from 1856 to 1861. In 1857, he was President of the Ninth Ward Republican Association, in 1858-59 he was Chairman of the Young Men's Republican Committee, and in 1860 he was President of the Wideawake Association. During the year last mentioned, he became a member of the Board of Supervisors of the County of New York. His business demanded his attention and there were other reasons why, in the fall of 1861, he moved to Brooklyn in order to sever his relations with that body. William M. Tweed was a member of the Board at that time, and began to develop some of the schemes which eventually caused his downfall. Mr. Dutcher was not willing to vote ignorantly on any question nor to act upon the representations of other members, who, he believed, held their personal interests above the interests of the county. As a resident of Brooklyn, he again resolved to keep out of politics, but the riots of 1863 brought him in close relations with active Republicans, and he found himself again in political harness. Nominated for Congress from the Second District of New York in 1870, he was defeated, although he proved his popularity by reducing the nominal Democratic majority in the district by about 4,000 and running about one thousand ahead of the Republican candidate for Governor.

He held the office of Supervisor of Internal Revenue 1868-1872, a period of four years, at first under appointment by Hugh McCulloch, the Secretary of the Treasury, and later under appointment by President Grant. In November, 1872, he was appointed United States Pension Agent, resigning that office in 1875 to accept a position in the employ of the Metropolitan Life Insurance Company, which he held until appointed United States Appraiser of the Port of New York by President Grant in March, 1877, which latter position he held until 1880. He was the Superintendent of Public Works of the State of New York, 1880-83, appointed by Governor Cornell. At the close of his term in the last named office, President Arthur requested him to accept the office of Commissioner of Internal Revenue, to which he replied that he had held office for fourteen years and all he had to show for that service was a few old clothes; that if he accepted the position tendered him and held it one or more years, he would retire with about the same quantity of old clothes as he had in the begining and so much older and less available for other business; and that the remainder of his life must be devoted to making some provision for his wife and children, and consequently he must decline further office-holding.

He was a member of the Charter Commission which framed the Charter of Greater New York, appointed by Governor Morton; and was appointed a manager of the Long Island State Hospital by Governor Black and re-appointed by Governor Roosevelt. He was a Whig from 1850 to 1855, and became a Republican at the organization of that party. After locating in Brooklyn, he was Chairman of the Kings County Republican Committee for four years; a member of the Republican State Committee for many years, and was Chairman of the Republican Executive Committee of the State in 1876. He served as a delegate to several Republican National Conventions and was on the stump in every presidential campaign from 1848 to 1888.

From the time he became a resident of Brooklyn until the consolidation was consummated, Mr. Dutcher was an advocate of the Consolidation of Brooklyn and New York. As a member for four years of the Brooklyn Board of Education, he exerted all his influence for the advancement of the public schools. As a member of the Charter Commission for Greater New York, he labored earnestly to secure equal taxation and home rule for the public schools, believing that the system and management in Brooklyn were better than in Manhattan, and better than any other in the proposed Greater New York. No work of his life has given him more satisfaction than the results in the charter on those two points. He has also taken an active interest in Sunday School affairs, and was Superintendent

EDITH M. DUTCHER

ELSIE R. (MRS. GILMOUR)

MRS. SILAS B. DUTCHER

JESSIE RUTH DUTCHER

EVA OLIVE DUTCHER

for ten years of the Twelfth Street Reformed Church Sunday School, at a time when it was one of the largest schools in the State.

Mr. Dutcher resumed business to some extent in 1885, when he formed a co-partnership with W. E. Edmister in a fire and marine insurance agency which still exists. He was one of the Charter Trustees of the Union Dime Savings Institution of New York City, organized 1859, and became President of that Institution in 1885, and is now the only one of the Charter Trustees remaining in the Board. He has been for twenty-five years a Director in the Metropolitan Life Insurance Company, is a member of the Chamber of Commerce, a Director in the Garfield Safe Deposit Company and the Goodwin Car Company.

He is a member of the Dutch Reformed Church, Treasurer of the Brooklyn Bible Society, one of the managers of the Society for Improving the Condition of the Poor, a member of the Brooklyn and Hamilton Clubs, and of the Masonic Fraternity, and he was President of the Association of Brooklyn Masonic Veterans in 1896.

In the spring of 1891, he was invited to and accepted the Presidency of the Hamilton Trust Company, which position he now holds. His residence is No. 496 Third Street, Brooklyn.

Mr. Dutcher has never been an applicant for any office that he has filled either under the Government or in private corporations.

The following editorial appeared in the Brooklyn Daily Eagle of July 12, 1899, and testifies to the position Mr. Dutcher has achieved and holds in the esteem and affections of the people of Brooklyn:

SEVENTY YEARS YOUNG.

"Those who have attained the age of seventy years, as a rule, attest the fact of a sound constitution and a well-spent life. The one is a fine inheritance. The other is a fine record. Inheritance and record both are the possession of the well-known Brooklynite, President Silas B. Dutcher of the Hamilton Trust Company. He was born seventy years ago to-day.

"He at once becomes a hope and a vindication. A hope he is to those who would equal his claim to respect and regard, who would match him in mental and bodily vigor, when they reach his present years. A vindication he is to those who seek for examples to prove that three score years and ten may be really the best period of a man's life. Mr. Dutcher very likely never thought of himself, either as a hope or as a vindication. He has been too busy to do so. That fact is one of the reasons why he is both. Life takes care of the fame of those who are more concerned with duty than distinction, for distinction is a consequence best following from fidelity, energy and wisdom. It is the aroma of a career, when the career is what it ought to be.

"The Eagle has obtained from Mr. Dutcher a pleasant and interesting statement of his experiences and of his opinions. What he says is very instructive. He was an effective school teacher, when school teaching was but a help toward something else. He was an employe of a railroad in a business capacity and that introduced him to more extended and fruitful employments. He well served others, until he acquired opportunity to become master of undertakings on his own account. And then important institutions in succession entrusted to his hands and brain the executive control of their own affairs. Increasing work seasoned his capacities. His character and ability together created and augmented in others confidence in him. But at no time, whether in public or business employments, has he let go of the sheet-anchor of a private business of his own. Influence and independence have thus gone hand-in-hand in his case.

"The man's political career has been one to note with respect. He has always acted with the organization of the party of his preference, but he has escaped the reproaches of that organization and every office which has come to him has added power to his party and assured honor to himself. Beside, he has never become dependent on political office. It has had grave need of him. He has not had vital need of it. Not that its emoluments have not been agreeable and helpful. They were, and they were as appreciated as deserved. But every public employment he has held has been a business employment. He filled every one in a way to prove his fitness for private employment. The portals of business opened to him often because of his efficiency in public service. His life exhibits a union or an alternation of public and private service which is creditable to citizenship.

"Moreover, he owed no start to favor or to relationship. He hewed his own path, made or found his own opportunities, and improved them as they came. But he did not neglect the better things than success, such as education, culture, and the other strengthening and graceful aids that stay by one forever, that render association refining, experience enlarging, intimacy uplifting, consultation helpful, reading a delight and leisure the recreation time of mind and heart. He is an accurate scholar, an effective speaker, a practical political economist, a wise counsellor, one who has reached the threshhold of age without a touch of grossness or a trace of vice or a hint of decrepitude.

"The Eagle congratulates him on his friendships and his years, and trusts that life may yet have many happy days and inciting duties in reserve for him."

Mr. Dutcher, on February 10, 1859, married Rebecca Jacobs Alwaise, born January 6, 1837, a daughter of John Alwaise of New York City, who was a grandson of John Alwaise, a French Huguenot who came to Philadelphia in 1740. Her grandmother was a descendant of John Bishop, who came from England in 1645 and settled at Woodbridge, New Jersey.

Mr. and Mrs. Silas Belden Dutcher have had eight children, as follows:

De Witt Parcefor, Edith May, Malcolm Belden, Elsie Rebecca, Myra Harriet, Jessie Ruth, Edna Grace and Eva Olive.

De Witt Parcefor, eldest son of Silas B. and Rebecca J. Dutcher, born at 51 Horatio St., New York City, March 18, 1860, married September 12, 1882, Grace Emily Furman, born September 8, 1860. He is a member of the Brooklyn City Guard, known as Company G, Twenty-third Regiment, National Guard, New York. He has been connected with that regiment for twenty-three years, during which period he has participated in all the service of the regiment, including duty in strikes at Buffalo, Brooklyn and Albany, and in many interesting celebrations, among which may be named, Centennial Evacuation Day Parade in 1883, the Bridge Opening in 1884, and the Quadri Centennial in 1893. He was also with his regiment at the funeral ceremonies of President U. S. Grant in New York in 1885.

He has been for twenty years in the General Appraiser's Department of the Federal Government.

Mr. and Mrs. De Witt P. Dutcher have children as follows:

Robert Roy Dutcher, born at Pearsalls, N. Y., May 26, 1884. He is a member of the Brooklyn City Guard, known as

DeWitt P. Dutcher

Grace E. Dutcher

Robert R. Dutcher

Myra H. Dutcher

Company G, Twenty-third Regiment National Guard, New York. At the age of fifteen, he paraded with the Twenty-third Regiment in the Admiral Dewey parade, marching directly in the rear of his father.

Myra Grace, born in Brooklyn, February 22, 1892.

They reside in their own house, No. 444 79th St., Brooklyn.

Edith May, second child of Silas B. and Rebecca J. Dutcher, born in Brooklyn, May 16, 1864.

She had a musical education and was for ten years the contralto soloist in two of the leading churches of Brooklyn.

Malcolm Belden, third child of Silas B. and Rebecca J. Dutcher, born in Brooklyn, February 22, 1873, married October 1, 1901, Edith Swarthout, born December 13, 1874.

He was graduated from the Civil Engineering course at the Polytechnic Institute at the age of nineteen, and immediately engaged in the business of Fire and Marine Insurance Brokerage.

He enlisted in Company C, Twenty-third Regiment, National Guard, New York, the same year, and was elected Lieutenant with the first change of Captain after his enlistment. He has participated in all the service of the regiment, including duty during the strikes in Brooklyn and Albany.

He has been active in Sunday School work and is Superintendent of the Sunday School of the Memorial Presbyterian Church.

Elsie Rebecca, fourth child of Silas B. and Rebecca J. Dutcher, born in Brooklyn, May 30, 1874, married November 10, 1896, Harvey J. Gilmour, born November 29, 1867. She has been a teacher in a Mission Sunday School for the past ten years.

Mr. and Mrs. Gilmour have one child:

Neil, born October 27, 1897.

Myra Harriet, fifth child of Silas B. and Rebecca J. Dutcher, born in Brooklyn, January 16, 1877, died September 20, 1892.

Jessie Ruth, sixth child of Silas Belden and Rebecca J Dutcher, born in Brooklyn, June 9, 1878. She was graduated from the Brooklyn High School and devotes much time to Sunday School work.

Edna Grace, twin daughter of Silas B. and Rebecca J. Dutcher, born in Brooklyn, February 15, 1880, died in Albany, March 10, 1882.

Eva Olive, twin daughter of Silas B. and Rebecca J. Dutcher, born in Brooklyn, February 15, 1880. She has been very studious, is especially fond of the dead languages, and was graduated from Barnard College in 1902.

Agnes Ann, third child of Parcefor Carr and Johannah Low (Frink) Dutcher, born April 2, 1836, at Springfield, Otsego County, N. Y., married at Senaca, Ontario County, N. Y., on September 22, 1857, Edward Root, born at Cazenovia, N. Y., March 24, 1829, died at Chittenango, N. Y., February 5, 1875.

Mrs. Root has been an invalid most of the time for the past ten years and much of that time unable to help herself in the slightest degree.

For five and a half years—from 1897 to 1902—she was most of the time utterly helpless, unable to make any use of her hands whatever, and was fed by others like a child. She was quite as helpless in her lower limbs. She had no hope of recovery and calmly awaited death to put an end to her sufferings and relieve her friends of the burden and care. In the early part of 1902 she began slowly

HARVEY J. GILMOUR

ELSIE R. GILMOUR née DUTCHER

NEIL GILMOUR

MALCOLM B DUTCHER

EDITH S DUTCHER

improving and gradually recovered the use of her hands and arms, so as to be able to feed herself and resume her old employments of knitting and sewing, and at the same time she partially recovered the use of her lower limbs. Her hopes were renewed and she began to feel that she had a new lease of life. She was overwhelmed with a sense of gratitude for this special mark of Divine favor. During her long period of suffering she was at all times an example of Christian patience and resignation. She could truthfully say, " For to live is Christ, to die is gain."

While her sufferings have been most severe, she is always cheerful, meeting her family and friends with a pleasant smile and ever yielding in humble submission to the Divine Will.

Mr. and Mrs. Root had children as follows:

Hannah Turner Root, John Dutcher Root, Alfred Edward Root.

Hannah Turner Root, eldest child of Edward and Agnes A. (Dutcher) Root, born May 9, 1859, at Cazenovia, died at Chittenango, December 30, 1889. She married Thomas Coon Bassett at Chittenango, N. Y., July 14, 1880. They had one child, Thomas Edward Bassett, born at Chittenango, May 18, 1881.

John Dutcher Root, second child of Edward and Agnes A. Root, born at Cazenovia, N. Y, April 19, 1862, married Lillie Ann Lawrence, November 4, 1885, at Oneida, New York. They have one child, Earl Comstock Root, born December, 1886.

Alfred Edward Root, youngest son of Edward and Agnes A. Root, born in Brooklyn, N. Y., October 26, 1863. He married Beatrice Kellogg Walrath, October 26, 1886, at Chittenango, N. Y., who died at Chittenango, N. Y., September 26, 1896. They had one child, Beatrice Kellogg Walrath Root, born at Chittenango, September 25, 1896, who died March 30, 1900.

Alfred Edward Root married Clara Alvira Morgan, his second wife, on August 9, 1899, at Cobleskill, N. Y.

Alfred Edward Root carries on a department store at Chittenango, N. Y.; his brother, John Dutcher Root is associated with him.

Harriet Elizabeth, youngest child of Parcefor Carr and Johannah Low (Frink) Dutcher, was born in Seneca, Ontario County, N. Y., on November 2, 1847.

The last fifteen years of her life were devoted to Hospital and Mission Service. She was graduated from the Bellevue Hospital Training School and was Matron of the Emergency Department of that Institution for two years. She was then called to the Sloan Maternity Hospital, which she opened, and of which she was Superintendent and Matron for five years, when her health failed. She then gave her attention wholly to mission work among the poor until she recovered her health.

In August, 1895, she became Matron and Superintendent of the Flushing Hospital, where she remained until her death on February 25, 1897.

The resolutions of the Board of Trustees and of the Medical Staff of the Flushing Hospital express the views of those who were most familiar with her work:

"FLUSHING, NEW YORK, March 8, 1897.

"At a meeting of the Trustees of the Hospital and Dispensary of the Town of Flushing held at this date, the following was unanimously adopted:

"WHEREAS, Miss Harriet E. Dutcher, who died February 25, 1897, was for nearly three years Matron of the Hospital and Dispensary of the Town of Flushing, and

"WHEREAS, During that time she rendered services of the greatest value, and greatly increased the effectiveness of the work of the Hospital, and by her devoted care of patients, her zealous co-operation with the Medical Staff, and her high character, general efficiency, amiability and unfailing cheerfulness, secured the respect, good will and affection of all persons with whom her work brought her into relations, Now therefore be it Resolved,

"That in her death, this Board and the Institution it represents have suffered an irreparable loss. That the members of her family have our sincere sympathy in their affliction, and that a copy of these resolutions be sent them by the Secretary, and entered upon the minutes of the Board. W. A. ALLEN, Secretary."

"At a meeting of the Medical Staff of the Flushing Hospital, held March 15, 1897, the following Preamble and Resolutions were unanimously adopted:

"WHEREAS, It has pleased Divine Providence to remove from us by death our trusted co-worker, associate and friend, Miss Harriet E. Dutcher, and we desiring to put upon record our deep sense of this loss, in each of these relations, it is therefore

"RESOLVED, That we each and all have in our close and pleasant association with Miss Dutcher learned how important an influence for good may emanate from a character so well poised, energetic and amiable as hers, and how practically essential these qualities are in promoting the purposes and maintaining the usefulness of such an institution as ours; and we feel that to attest to these qualities and to proclaim this result, is the debt and the duty we owe to her memory:

"RESOLVED, The Staff desires to express to the members of her family and her friends their deep sympathy in the loss and bereavement that has come upon them, and to join with all in the confident assurance that a life so good, so useful, so rounded out in beauty of character, is at once an influence and a gift to all who knew her, enduring and fruitful.

"Resolved, that these resolutions be entered upon the minutes of this Board, that a copy of the same be transmitted to the family of the deceased, and that they be published in the Flushing Journal.

Dr. E. A. Goodrich,   J. L. Hicks
    President Medical Board.   Secretary.
Dr. E. A. Allen,   Dr. Bloodgood,
Dr. Bleecker,   Dr. Lawrence."

Her profession gave her a large acquaintance and all who knew her held her in the highest esteem.